Sixty Women Poets

edited by

LINDA FRANCE

BLOODAXE BOOKS

ISBN: 1 85224 252 3

First published 1993 by
Bloodaxe Books Ltd,
P.O. Box 1SN,
Newcastle upon Tyne NE99 1SN.

Bloodaxe Books Ltd acknowledges
the financial assistance of Northern Arts.

*For Anabel, Hilary, Jan, Pauline,
Rosemary, Sarah, Susie and Lorna.*

Cover printing by J. Thomson Colour Printers Ltd, Glasgow.

Printed in Great Britain by
Bell & Bain Limited, Glasgow, Scotland.

SIXTY WOMEN POETS

Linda France was born in 1958 in Newcastle. After living in Dorset, Leeds, London and Amsterdam, she returned to the North East in 1981, and now lives in Hexham. She has two children and works as a freelance writer and part-time tutor in adult education. She won the Basil Bunting Award in 1988 and 1989. She appeared in the ITV poetry series *Wordworks*, and wrote and appeared in *Fire and Brimstone*, a poetry and music collaboration based on the life of the artist John Martin. Her first book of poems, *Red*, was published by Bloodaxe Books in 1992; her second, *The Gentleness of the Very Tall*, is forthcoming in 1994. She is the editor of the Bloodaxe anthology *Sixty Women Poets* (1993).

CONTENTS

The editor regrets that Sheenagh Pugh was not willing to be represented in this book because she refuses to have her poetry published in women's anthologies.

INTRODUCTION

This anthology follows in the non-exclusive tradition already established by, among others, Carol Rumens' *Making for the Open* (Chatto, 1985), Jeni Couzyn's *Bloodaxe Book of Contemporary Women Poets* (1985) and Fleur Adcock's *Faber Book of Twentieth Century Women's Poetry* (1987). It also occupies and overlaps the space between these and Carol Rumens' *New Women Poets* (Bloodaxe, 1990).

I see it also as a necessary sister volume to Bloodaxe's *The New Poetry* (1993), which editors Michael Hulse, David Kennedy and David Morley claim represents 'the best poetry written in the British Isles in the 1980s and early 1990s by a distinctive new generation of poets'. While it is hardly surprising that out of 55 poets, only 17 women are included by an all-male editorial team, their selection cannot be taken as an accurate or adequate reflection of what is going on in poetry in the period covered, given the evident strengths of the work of the younger women poets represented *here*. Ghettoising and separatism are not options I willingly court, nor is it part of my intention to exclude or alienate the male reader. It has long been unnecessary to justify an anthology of women's poetry on grounds of gender alone. However, it is regrettable that this will continue to be the case while women poets continue to be unfairly represented in mixed gender "canonical" anthologies.

Stevie Smith died in 1971, and I have taken that as a starting date, honouring her influence and importance. This allowed me to include an older generation of women poets who have been forgotten or neglected, such as Freda Downie and Ruth Pitter, as well as those who are still writing and publishing, like Elizabeth Jennings, Jenny Joseph, E.J. Scovell and Anne Stevenson. Many women are unable to take themselves seriously as writers until they reach a certain age, with the waning of family commitments alongside the waxing of self-confidence and considered abandon. The poets I have chosen to include fall loosely into three generations, grandmothers, mothers and daughters (in the creative rather than procreative sense), a natural and appropriate layering. The different voices do not jar; rather they enhance one another and the distinction according to birth date ceases to matter. Hence the decision to organise the book in alphabetical order of poet rather than by age. Neither the intention nor the effect is one of linearity.

Although all the poets have been published in Britain or Ireland, many have either non-British origins or strong connections with other parts of the world, reflecting the geographical flux of contemporary society. Those North American poets who have chosen to make their home here, Julie O'Callaghan, Anne Rouse and Eva Salzman, bring more than the ambiguous privilege of the outsider, the sideways look to contemporary women's poetry. The rhythms and allusions of their various vernaculars are simultaneously unusual and familiar. Their differences provide a rich source for the trawling and teasing out of illusion and its opposite.

Poetic activity among women writers in Ireland is another important element in the current milieu. The poets themselves have spoken of a sense of revival and it is present in the work, represented here by selections from Nuala Archer, Leland Bardwell, Eavan Boland, Eiléan Ní Chuilleanáin, Nuala Ní Dhomhnaill, Rita Ann Higgins, Medbh McGuckian and Paula Meehan. The emphatic restrictions imposed by both Church and State in Ireland have resulted in a powerful poetry of resistance. The work is intense and vigorous, uncompromising in its femaleness, satisfying in its humour and tender in the lyricism of the "mother tongue".

One of the original criteria for inclusion was that the poets should have had at least two collections published. However that involved excluding many of the new voices introduced by *New Women Poets* who have gone on to publish impressive and exciting first collections, notably Elizabeth Garrett, Lavinia Greenlaw, Jackie Kay, Mimi Khalvati, Anne Rouse and Eva Salzman. Moniza Alvi, not included in *New Women Poets*, is represented here with poems from her first collection, containing elements of East and West, seen also to good effect in the work of Sujata Bhatt and Mimi Khalvati. A similar cultural interplay is reflected in the concerns of Caribbean poets Jean 'Binta' Breeze and Grace Nichols.

It was important to me to include work by new younger poets to give this anthology a sense of the moment, of hard currency, as well as surveying the decades post-1971. A sense of history occurs in the work itself, reaching further back in time in the settings of poems in Classical Greece, Medieval France, Jacobite and Victorian England, Europe during the Wars and the America of Bessie Smith and the Ku Klux Klan. Women have the ability it seems almost physically to inhabit history and the passage of time, as much in the wider historical sense as in the way it is experienced in their own lives and those of their families, their parents' generations and their children's.

The selection of poets is necessarily based upon my own assessment of what makes a poem a good one. Applying criteria of "quality" is inevitably a fraught exercise; however, I have chosen only those poems that I feel successfully order thought, emotion and imagination into a form that communicates itself effectively and unequivocally to the reader. Or if speculation or ambivalence are part of the poem's source, that is conveyed to the reader too.

Much of the poetry written by women since 1971 appears either directly or indirectly to derive from a radical requirement to balance contradictory or opposing forces, charting how these arise in a dangerous and demanding world and how the poets as women experience them, attempt to make sense of them and then go on to deal with them. Some of these conflicts are certainly human ones but there are plenty more that are associated with the female experience within a patriarchy. In the poetry as in the life the clashes occur on both inner and outer levels. Perfect poise is difficult to achieve, even more difficult to maintain, and is deftly thrown out of kilter simply by the movement of the world turning. However, the poems themselves can, and do, struggle for balance, achieve it and hold it in place as a reminder of what is possible. Medbh McGuckian addresses this issue in her sensuous and original, occasionally disarming, poetry, which challenges received notions of reality and established forms, not least by her use of a non-linear syntax. The effect is 'A Different Same', a counterpoint of the rich and seductive and the painful and elusive, a very striking marriage of heaven and hell. Living as she does in Belfast, her striving towards peace and resolution takes on even deeper resonances.

These women poets, despite their different viewpoints, share similar observations, and to varying degrees accept the contradictions of a well-lived life, the experience of paradox, whether they like it or not. This is to return to the concept of non-linearity: life as repeating cycles, containing dark as well as light, bad and good, male and female. What is new here is that these opposing forces are seen as co-existing, part of the same whole; as if duality has been exposed as yet another inherited out-worn tradition, used too frequently to divide rather than to unite.

For a woman, whatever the gender of the muse, the process of responding openly to and interacting with her imagination is as redemptive as it is imperative. The work of these poets seems to me to reveal an error in Yeats's declaration that the artist has to make a choice between a good life and good art. The honesty of a clearly owned 'I' in this poetry, which has the effect of extending the boundaries of autobiography further and further past traditional English embarrassment, is an act of courage and commitment. Women are now finding themselves in a position to take both their lives and their poetry seriously; the two need not be separate. This is just one of the many positive results of the Women's Movement and the work that women have been engaged in both together and alone during the past two decades. Feminism did not die under the rule of Britain's first woman Prime Minister. But what should have been a blessing turned out to be a curse; and not only for women.

This is not to suggest that following an active, constructive dialectic is easy, or that women poets are dealing with their struggles, political, personal and creative, in an unrealistic, high-minded, ascetic way. What the poetry reflects is 'the accumulation of small acts of kindness' and the 'inside of pleasure' that enhance a life, the positive principle in action. The pleasure principle has its place here too. More than ever before the erotic is available to women as theme or metaphor. The poetry often has a wild quality, the sense of a creature constrained too long, wanting to taste earthy pleasures, untrammelled by the still cautious eyes of a culture fuelled by guilt and containment.

The erotic is both subject and object in work by Sujata Bhatt, Carol Ann Duffy, Selima Hill, Sylvia Kantaris, Grace Nichols, Deborah Randall and Penelope Shuttle. However, in these and other cases it eludes its narrow sexual definition, extending to an awareness and engagement of all five senses and the effect upon the imagination, as well as the body. This is part of a well-documented female tradition traced back to Sappho and flourishing, despite centuries of oppression, in the work of poets like Aphra Behn, Christina Rossetti and Edna St Vincent Millay. What is happening is not new but the directness and sheer abundance of it can sometimes make it feel so.

All these elements contained in women's poetry now function against a background of much laughter, at many different pitches, skilled in irony and parody as well as the big joke, the belly-laugh. Much of the work of Wendy Cope, Selima Hill and U.A. Fanthorpe is both intelligent and witty, willing and able to dramatise the tragic as well as the comic in a playful and affirming way. Humour is a part of the new openness, the new opportunities available to women writers. It is directly connected with an accessibility of voice and themes reflected in work that is as successful in performance as it is on the page. The popularity of the

extremely enjoyable and skilful readings by poets like Liz Loch-
head and Jackie Kay, amongst others, reveals a powerful demand
to hear how the poems sound, to share the active, live experience
of women's creativity.

This is how I see the guiding force behind this anthology:
women being positive, creative and in control of their own lives.
Not in a falsely complacent sense of all the battles being won, a new
post-feminist dawn. Although I do think that the battle lines have
shifted and are shifting. Anything could happen and probably will.
By being true to their own natures, women are pursuing empathy,
a traditionally feminine quality too easily demeaned and abused.
Alongside a more passive sensitivity, there is a distinctly active
aspect revealed in this poetry, a spirit of adventure, curiosity and
exploration. The blend is a potent one, shooting sparks in many
directions.

The importance of charting and celebrating what can be seen as
a renaissance in women's poetry, the vital and positive work that
women are currently engaged in, lies in the sustenance and sup-
port it provides for the growing numbers of women reading poetry
as well as those engaged in the business of writing it, whether
intended for publication or not. The traditional female skills nec-
essary for managing and nourishing the extended family, the exig-
encies of participating in a community, have been carried over into
the way women campaign politically, for general social and environ-
mental issues as well as specifically for women's rights. This "net-
working" occurs on artistic levels too, in both organised and infor-
mal ways. The sense of place, of community, is an important one
and I hope this anthology finds its own point of balance in that
sharing and mirroring. We can only truthfully make the books we
want to read, remembering and responding to everything that we've
read before and what it meant to us, how it changed how we see
ourselves and the world we live in. Despite our differences, our
concerns are essentially very similar. The same themes occur: love,
death, work, family, childhood, art, time, memory, place, nourish-
ment and dreams; above all, transformative acts of the imagination.

The impulse of empathy is seen most directly in the way these
poets are so adept at inhabiting other voices. Carol Ann Duffy's
facility with the monologue has been rightly praised. In this selec-
tion she speaks through a maidservant engaged in the seductive
ritual of warming her mistress's pearls as well as from the stand-
point of an artist's model able dispassionately to observe the
artist's process and the finished portrait that fails to capture her

sense of herself. Other poets are seen here bravely taking on the imperatives of the male voice as well as a wide range of imaginary or historical female figures. Not to mention at least one dragon.

The voices vary as much as the themes, from the elegant lyricism of Elaine Feinstein and Pauline Stainer, through the self-possessed intelligence of Lavinia Greenlaw and Jo Shapcott, to the sensuous individualism of Sujata Bhatt, Selima Hill and Deborah Randall. A formal awareness is present even in the work of those poets who apparently eschew tradition. However, all these poets have dexterity at their disposal. Many choose to make use of traditional form to forceful effect, while still managing to make of it something new, something more than simply an arrangement of lines carved by tradition; it is substance and sinew, essential to the poem's unique meaning. What is refreshing is that there is never any sense of the merely ephemeral, of fashion, "schools" where these poets have served their time. The poets are confident enough to be their own women and that includes experimentation with technique in pursuit of an integrity of practice, born of more energetic application than is generally acknowledged. The work of Elizabeth Bartlett is a case in point. Her striking use of narrative voice to achieve a sense of dislocation, to stretch the boundaries of the imagination, was appearing in her work long before post-modernism became the right car to be seen to drive.

The French writer Marguerite Duras has said 'The truth is what I think sometimes, on some days about some things.' I perceive the same awareness echoed in the work of these sixty women poets. Rather than suggesting evasion, the poetry shows that this involves an active recognition of the implications of change and an unflinching commitment to the discovery and celebration of 'What is worth knowing'. Anne Stevenson also points out why, as well as what is worth avoiding:

> evade the ego-hill, the misery-well,
> the siren hiss of *publish, success, publish,*
> *success, success, success*
>
> And why inhabit, make, inherit poetry?
>
> Oh, it's the shared comedy of the worst
> blessed, the sound leading the hand;
> a wordlife running from mind to mind
> through the washed rooms of the simple senses;
> one of those haunted, undefendable, unpoetic
> crosses we have to find.

FLEUR ADCOCK

Against Coupling

I write in praise of the solitary act:
of not feeling a trespassing tongue
forced into one's mouth, one's breath
smothered, nipples crushed against the
ribcage, and that metallic tingling
in the chin set off by a certain odd nerve:

unpleasure. Just to avoid those eyes would help –
such eyes as a young girl draws life from,
listening to the vegetal
rustle within her, as his gaze
stirs polypal fronds in the obscure
sea-bed of her body, and her own eyes blur.

There is much to be said for abandoning
this no longer novel exercise –
for not 'participating in
a total experience' – when
one feels like the lady in Leeds who
had seen *The Sound of Music* eighty-six times;

or more, perhaps, like the school drama mistress
producing *A Midsummer Night's Dream*
for the seventh year running, with
yet another cast from 5B.
Pyramus and Thisbe are dead, but
the hole in the wall can still be troublesome.

I advise you, then, to embrace it without
encumbrance. No need to set the scene,
dress up (or undress), make speeches.
Five minutes of solitude are
enough – in the bath, or to fill
that gap between the Sunday papers and lunch.

Future Work

'Please send future work'
                    – EDITOR'S NOTE ON A REJECTION SLIP

It is going to be a splendid summer.
The apple tree will be thick with golden russets
expanding weightily in the soft air.
I shall finish the brick wall beside the terrace
and plant out all the geranium cuttings.
Pinks and carnations will be everywhere.

She will come out to me in the garden,
her bare feet pale on the cut grass,
bringing jasmine tea and strawberries on a tray.
I shall be correcting the proofs of my novel
(third in a trilogy – simultaneous publication
in four continents); and my latest play

will be in production at the Aldwych
starring Glenda Jackson and Paul Scofield
with Olivier brilliant in a minor part.
I shall probably have finished my translations
of Persian creation myths and the Pre-Socratics
(drawing new parallels) and be ready to start

on Lucretius. But first I'll take a break
at the chess championships in Manila –
on present form, I'm fairly likely to win.
And poems? Yes, there will certainly be poems:
they sing in my head, they tingle along my nerves.
It is all magnificently about to begin.

Things

There are worse things than having behaved foolishly in public.
There are worse things than these miniature betrayals
committed or endured or suspected; there are worse things
than not being able to sleep for thinking about them.
It is 5 a.m. All the worse things come stalking in
and stand icily about the bed looking worse and worse and worse.

The Keepsake
(in memory of Pete Laver)

'To Fleur from Pete, on loan perpetual.'
It's written on the flyleaf of the book
I wouldn't let you give away outright:
'Just make it permanent loan' I said – a joke
between librarians, professional
jargon. It seemed quite witty, on a night

when most things passed for wit. We were all hoarse
by then, from laughing at the bits you'd read
aloud – the heaving bosoms, blushing sighs,
demoniac lips. 'Listen to this!' you said:
' "Thus rendered bold by frequent intercourse
I dared to take her hand." ' We wiped our eyes.

' "Colonel, what mean these stains upon your dress?" '
We howled. And then there was Lord Ravenstone
faced with Augusta's dutiful rejection
in anguished prose; or, for a change of tone,
a touch of Gothic: Madame la Comtesse
's walled-up lover. An inspired collection:

The Keepsake, 1835; the standard
drawing-room annual, useful as a means
for luring ladies into chaste flirtation
in early 19th century courtship scenes.
I'd never seen a copy; often wondered.
Well, here it was – a pretty compilation

of tales and verses: stanzas by Lord Blank
and Countess This and Mrs That; demure
engravings, all white shoulders, corkscrew hair
and swelling bosoms; stories full of pure
sentiments, in which gentlemen of rank
urged suits upon the nobly-minded fair.

You passed the volume round, and poured more wine.
Outside your cottage lightning flashed again:
a Grasmere storm, theatrically right
for stories of romance and terror. Then
somehow, quite suddenly, the book was mine.
The date in it's five weeks ago tonight.

'On loan perpetual.' If that implied
some dark finality, some hint of 'nox
perpetua', something desolate and bleak,
we didn't see it then, among the jokes.
Yesterday, walking on the fells, you died.
I'm left with this, a trifling, quaint antique.

You'll not reclaim it now; it's mine to keep:
a keepsake, nothing more. You've changed the 'loan
perpetual' to a bequest by dying.
Augusta, Lady Blanche, Lord Ravenstone –
I've read the lot, trying to get to sleep.
The jokes have all gone flat. I can't stop crying.

Counting

You count the fingers first: it's traditional.
(You assume the doctor counted them too,
when he lifted up the slimy surprise
with its long dark pointed head and its father's nose
at 2.13 a.m. – 'Look at the clock!'
said Sister: 'Remember the time: 2.13.')

Next day the head's turned pink and round;
the nose is a blob. You fumble under the gown
your mother embroidered with a sprig of daisies,
as she embroidered your own Viyella gowns
when you were a baby. You fish out
curly triangular feet. You count the toes.

'There's just one little thing' says Sister:
'His ears – they don't quite match. One
has an extra whorl in it. No one will notice.'
You notice like mad. You keep on noticing.
Then you hear a rumour: a woman in the next ward
has had a stillbirth. Or was it something worse?

You lie there, bleeding gratefully.
You've won the Nobel Prize, and the VC,
and the State Lottery, and gone to heaven.
Feed-time comes. They bring your bundle –
the right one: it's him all right.
You count his eyelashes: the ideal number.

You take him home. He learns to walk.
From time to time you eye him,
nonchalantly, from each side.
He has an admirable nose.
No one ever notices his ears. No one
ever stands on both sides of him at once.

He grows up. He has beautiful children.

GILLIAN ALLNUTT

Ode

To depict a (bicycle), you must first come to love (it).
ALEXANDER BLOK

I swear by every rule in the bicycle
owner's manual

that I love you, I, who have repeatedly,
painstakingly,

with accompanying declaration of despair,
tried to repair

you, to patch things up,
to maintain a workable relationship.

I have spent sleepless nights
in pondering your parts – those private

and those that all who walk the street
may look at –

wondering what makes you tick
over smoothly, or squeak.

O my trusty steed,
my rusty three-speed,

I would feed you the best oats
if oats

were applicable.
Only linseed oil

will do
to nourish you.

I want
so much to paint

you,
midnight blue

mudgutter black
and standing as you do, ironic

at the rail
provided by the Council –

beautiful
the sun caught in your back wheel –

or at home in the hall, remarkable
among other bicycles,

your handlebars erect.
Allow me to depict

you thus. And though I can't do justice
to your true opinion of the surface

of the road –
put into words

the nice distinctions that you make
among the different sorts of tarmac –

still I'd like to set the record of our travels straight.
I'd have you know that

not with three-in-one
but with my own

heart's
spittle I anoint your moving parts.

convent

a fistful of notes
my heart

a thin must
covers the keyboard of ivory soldiers

girls are expected
to wear gloves

and a labour of love is lost
in plain sewing

each finger stitched
to the palm

the loose hem of the street
catches me

the tune
of a barrel organ

the monkey
playing alone

streetheart
no penny can buy it

I ought
to give my pocket

money for a poor child
going begging in the east

in the name of the father the son
and the monkey goes on

like the ghost
of a tell tale tit your heart shall be split

while the bell rings for angelus
here are gloves of silk a purse

on a string
worn over the shoulder

and nothing
in it

after prayers
there will be bread and butter soldiers

a measure of milk
plainsong

heart note

because we for a while had been living there my heart

thought it was a house with cupboards and an open fire
and a door giving onto
an impossible steep twisted stair my heart

thought it could have small uncurtained windows it could go on
being there under its tiles for the swallows
every year

love was already living in the house my heart

thought when we got there it thought it was
a letterbox a back door opening to
a garden it could walk in

it was nothing we had put there but before us it was

apple willow and a wilderness of
rose thorn thick and dark
and light with its daylong delicate flowers my heart

thought it had roots it thought it could cover its roots
with straw it thought it could carry on
lighting its every morning fire

because we as love for a while had been living there

About Benwell

Perhaps there will always be yellow buses
passing and Presto's
and people with faces like broken promises

and shops full of stotties and butties and buckets and bubble bath
and bones for broth
where the poor may inherit the earth

and women who will
wade into the wind and waste with hope eternal
and kids like saplings planted by the Council

and Thomas Armstrong's endless line
of bairns, whose names, in sandstone,
rehabilitate their streets of rag and bone

where bits of paper, bottle tops and Pepsi cans blow up and down
despondently, like souls on their own.
Perhaps there will always be unremembered men

and maps of Old Dunston and Metroland and the rough blown rain
and the riding down of the sun
towards Blaydon.

MONIZA ALVI

I Would Like to be a Dot in a Painting by Miró

I would like to be a dot in a painting by Miró.

Barely distinguishable from other dots,
it's true, but quite uniquely placed.
And from my dark centre

I'd survey the beauty of the linescape
and wonder – would it be worthwhile
to roll myself towards the lemon stripe,

Centrally poised, and push my curves
against its edge, to get myself
a little extra attention?

But it's fine where I am.
I'll never make out what's going on
around me, and that's the joy of it.

The fact that I'm not a perfect circle
makes me more interesting in this world.
People will stare forever –

Even the most unemotional get excited.
So here I am, on the edge of animation,
a dream, a dance, a fantastic construction,

A child's adventure.
And nothing in this tawny sky
can get too close, or move too far away.

The Sari

Inside my mother
I peered through a glass porthole.
The world beyond was hot and brown.

They were all looking in on me –
Father, Grandmother,
the cook's boy, the sweeper-girl,
the bullock with the sharp
shoulderblades,
the local politicians.

My English grandmother
took a telescope
and gazed across continents.

All the people unravelled a sari.
It stretched from Lahore to Hyderabad,
wavered across the Arabian Sea,
shot through with stars,
fluttering with sparrows and quails.
They threaded it with roads,
undulations of land.

Eventually
they wrapped and wrapped me in it
whispering *Your body is your country*.

Map of India

If I stare at the country long enough
I can prise it off the paper,
lift it like a flap of skin.

Sometimes it's an advent calendar –
each city has a window
which I leave open
a little wider each time.

India is manageable – smaller than
my hand, the Mahanadi River
thinner than my lifeline.

On Finding a Letter to Mrs Vickers
on the Pennine Way

A bird with a torn tail hops under ferns
and points its beak to the wall.

A letter to Mrs Vickers is trodden into the path –
colours have run into edges soft as cotton.

Mrs Vickers, Mrs Vickers
you have won, you have almost won
a Ford Escort. We of the Prizes Department
are sending you a draft of the Award Certificate.

Earth trickles over it like a child's pattern.

Mrs Vickers, calling your number at Stoneway
we would like to tell you
you're in with a winning chance.
Don't miss the cellophane window.

It shines like a dirty film of ice.

Mrs Vickers, don't forget to tell us
all about yourself.
Then tread this well into the path
where the mossy fronds dart like fishes –

And the bird fans out its broken tail.

NUALA ARCHER

Whale on the Line
(for John)

1

You can't hear me dialling your number
because a whale is tangled
in the telephone cables on the ocean floor.
For some unknown reason

he torpedoed to the bottom. Cables entwine
the spool of his body — forty-five tons
of blubber the colour of your blue eyes.
His last air bubbles drift up

like small parachutes. He explores
the darkness by ear, listens
to kelp wave solemnly back and forth
like ushers at a funeral.

It took the scuba divers
days of overtime to unknot the mesh.
Arc lamps scattered light
in strange shadows. A white octopus

floated about, curling and uncurling
his arms like yo-yo's, gently touching
the whale's slack muscles,
open mouth and lidded eyes.

2

For months words drift in shoals
around the quiet whale…'Remember
nightingales, stars, hibiscus, the late
train, willows of wind…?'

Fish gargoyles, carrying lamps,
pick barnacles off the whale's back.
Submarine gulls circle and scream
Ballena! Ballena! Kujira! Kujira!

The whale's skull lies in sand.
A seaweed tongue flutters with the tide.
His stoney ears patiently become
the water sounding against a calf

just born to blue-green September
light. Soft explosions of breath
buoy her thermos-shaped body.
An albatross wraps the five-foot cord

around its neck, tears into placenta
as a clean wind tears clouds open.
Half-awake the calf rolls with the slanting
sea into a night brightened by the moon's

rainbow witches. Fog horns call back memories
of ships – *Union, Essex, Ann Alexander*
and *Kathleen* – sent to the bottom by whales;
and of whales lashed to my call of love for you.

Towards Another Terminal

Down silver eels
the train highballs
into the iron barn.
Its whistle moans
to the red-haired moon
as Ms Fashoon sidles over
to Walter and a vodka gimlet.

Her eyes are strawberries
with green lashes.
She is a tall coyote
trying to bite her heart into
digestible pieces.
'Please,' she says,
'where's my man, where's the next
whistle blowing from, where
are my shoes in relation
to my head, will you be my
new earring?'

The train scribbles
a blackboard sky, its white
eye whips
the glittering rails
towards another terminal.

Rocking
(for Mary L.)

These days I wake up crying
holding myself in my arms
rocking myself like a mother
repeating
it's all right – i'm here.
And the room I wake up in
rocks in the arms that are rocking
me. The walls move
like a sea ebbing and flowing.
They never rest and all the books
with their thousands of pages
and millions of words
which I can hardly read
move to the rhythm or
a hammock pushed by the indifferent
toe of a Cuna mother,
who is I, as she prods the
open fire and sings *nanas*
of sound which are not English
yet echo in my ear like
the surf in a shell.
The lamp on the desk and
all the pencils and the black,
golden-eyed kitten
looking at me – all move
to and fro with the room
swaying through space like
a pendulum that has swung into orbit,
spiralling now closer,
now farther away, and the

nails that fixed the room and me
to a place seem to be flying
in all directions

and I rock myself
and I rock myself
and the room rocks me
until I find my feet again
and can walk, learning to let go.

ANNEMARIE AUSTIN

Night Bus

You have to hold on to your faith in a world outside;
that, where the road bends here, the thin copse lifts
its fingers of trees in the dark, half shielding the field beyond
where three horses always graze, the two dappled, the one brown.

For no one looks in at the window save your own ghost
keeping pace. You press your shoulder up against the darkness
that presses its shoulder up against the glass. There is nothing
to be seen past dried mud splashes like grey feathers.

And you know there could be anything out there: the bus
is lurching on a knife-edge ridge, precipices right and left;
or that you and your companions never left the garage
but wait in a windowless hangar with the engine revved.

Shape-shifting

You see the same face across the generations –
her there, half a shadow and half concrete
in a real coat with mud-flecked facings,
a fraying hem, and lugging a leather suitcase
tied with string. She sings the same thread song

that her mother whispered above her cradle
in the winter dark about a thousand years ago;
the look in her eyes dissolves into a landscape
puddled with mud, far trees against the sky
and a rider going between them – herself maybe.

For she rises up wherever you might be watching
in a different costume, with various coloured hair
or lion's pelt, bird feathers – your glance catches
her even in the fireside cat that licks its paws
then turns its flexing gaze towards your face

before stalking out to the dusk and its dissolving.
And she is there at the gate, unlatching it and entering,
leaving her horse by the fence, feeling the cat's fur cold
against her legs as she advances up the shadowed path
to temporary safety. A woman within a home

for the briefest moment, she boils a kettle at the fire,
hangs her frayed coat on a peg and hunkers down
before the hearth to sing for anything arriving
out of the old winter dark – the gold-leaf lion
hauling a leather suitcase, a peacock trailing string.

Clothing

There should be, I assume, some correlation
between each object and the desire it calls
to itself, like moon dragging tides along behind;
but perhaps, they say, you are not so very weighty,
I've clothed you in layers like an onion's coats,
desire on desire, distorting your living centre
where the green shoot waits its moment, nearly stifled.

I don't know. Nightly dreams increase the freight,
complexity, compile a past we do not really share
in every kind of setting, every age; the huge weight
of them pulls on the neck and shoulders, hunching
both of us; we are attired for several Arctic winters.
Yet at the grain of the snowball, somewhere,
there is essential you, the person where I started.

Smaller perhaps, compacted, distillation of the colours
I have spread to make you from, taking less space
in passages and hallways, surrounded by less air
and echo everywhere, quieter; crowds do not part
inevitably letting you through nor do admirers gather
for your arrival... except me, equipped for snowman-
building with half at least a cloakroom's worth of coats.

Pen and Paper

Before the ladder to the platform closed in by fleering voices,
the tying of the feet, the laying on the tilted board face down
but with no place for cheek or lip to rest on,
before the oblique blade, the bloody basket;
arrived at the foot of the scaffold, Madame Roland asked
that she might have pen and paper to record
'the strange thoughts rising in her'.
                                        Request refused,
as if it were some clever-dick trick of postponement;
the page remaining at the stationers, the quill untrimmed,
the strange thoughts in the skull as in a vase
that spilt them quite illegibly under the guillotine
a moment later.
                        A fate she knew could not be much delayed,
she would not read her own words back to her
at leisure after, what she felt urged to keep
could not be kept by her more than a minute's space;
but nonetheless she wanted pen and paper, meant
to snatch out of the blood-stained air those phrases
that would cage the strangeness lifting through her now.

For only words could net and hold the foreign birds
long enough in her sight for naming, recognition
under the single lightning-flash that time had left her;
only with pen and paper could she possess her death,
the momentary owner of a basket loud with wings
that the imminent blow would knock from her hands and scatter.

LELAND BARDWELL

Husbands

My first husband hated intelligent women
he thought they were like avocado pears,
expensive, tasteless.

He said if I was let loose
I might go to Mexico
although his horizons
were leather skirts.

My second husband hated Mexicans
and me. He said we had ended the transfer.
He liked Antonioni women
with short hair and big bums
and wanted to be one.

I'd like a new one with no hatreds
and superb teeth.
Both my husbands had grey smiles
and were transvestites.

I thought that stupid
(so what if my breasts
are like two fried eggs?)
They haven't any.

I was once screwed in Euston Station
and saw mercury running.
If I could have bottled it
I'd have made a fortune.

First

A dog should die outside, the others said
but I had taken her
scrunched up in my arms,
hidden her in the shed.

We lay together in a shroud of hay
holding death aside
like the curtain in a theatre.
But then it came: the blood.
It spurted from her mouth,
spurted on the flagstones
like a string of beads.

What follows obliterates,
with each new loss,
that accident of grief.
But how can one forget what was one's
first. First anything, first love,
first loss, first kiss.

Pointless

You go on and on.

But imagine the world without music.
Just imagine – no fifths, no thirds,
no arpeggios, no atonal notes.
(And surely God invented the octave.)

I once saw a horse dance in Phoenix Park.

Yes you go on and on
saying art, unless political, is pointless.
But you don't pick blackberries with me
you are not interested in mud.

Children's Games
(for William and Anna Bardwell)

Once upon a time
I saw my two children playing
where Karl Marx was lying
with a tombstone on his head;
they were naked from the waist down

and the English around and around said
Better the children dead
than naked from the waist down

Now I was a foreigner
on that cold Highgate Hill
but I bore no ill to the English
no ill

So I toiled away by the Spaniards
where the English were all lovers
and their legs gleamed O
so cold and naked
naked from the waist down

and I tried another graveyard
and found another plot
where Sigmund Freud was lying
in his eiderdown of weeds

My children, I said, romp away
this little strip is yours
for the dead are mostly idle
and do not care if you are naked
naked from the waist down

and the graves began to smile
and the hymn of England fade
and my children took out their pocket knives
and carved on the limey stone:

Dr Freud lies here in the nettles
we are dancing on his head

Lila's Potatoes

They asked me to write a poem
about Lila's potatoes
I thought about the eighteen forties
I thought about watercress
I thought about weeds
but they were black
my plants were black
lazy beds, they said, were OK.

I had spent my life in lazy beds
one way and another – lazy beds
in and out of lazy beds.

They'd got me everywhere
when I slept in different towns,
places, seas, – another child
lazy beds, they said, were OK in the famine.

I saw my plants – black – leaves black
stalks black – lazy beds, they said –
in the famine – lazy beds.

So I made kids in lazy beds – strapping women
all all from lazy beds – eight altogether
they got jobs in underground London pubs,
strip halls – make-believe – run around
and ended up in lazy beds all eight of them.

Lazy beds make black potatoes – Lila's potatoes
have the blight – lazy beds – Lila's potatoes
they got the blight.

Then Seamus took the bad luck out of it.
It was the sun, he said, caused it.
I often wondered what caused all my children.
I'm glad it was the sun.

ELIZABETH BARTLETT

There Is a Desert Here

I loved you in silence, without hope, jealous and afraid.
PUSHKIN

There is a desert here I cannot travel,
There is sand I cannot tip from my shoes.
Over my left eyebrow is a greenish bruise.
There is you, and there is me. I cannot choose
But love you, though you wrong me,
And make angry love to me, a smack
Like a caress, a careless move, and a crack
Appears in your loving, widening, widening.
It was a bad bargain I made with you.
Your green eyes and your strutting maturity
Did not mix well with my long pale face
And my convent innocence, but they looked
At me, flashes of light, like sexual lightning,
Blackening my tree. At last I sprout
From the bole after all these years
When you might have thought my tears
Were gone, and my tortured tree was dead.

Come little creatures, walk on me,
Come little worms, slide upon me,
For no man ever will again.
I watched beetles and ladybirds
Long before you gathered birch twigs
To beat me in a field – in fun, of course,
And I will watch them again,
And grow old ungracefully, barefoot
And sluttish in my ways.
No more hauling of ashes,
I promise you.

God Is Dead – Nietzsche

Daddy and I are always here, you know,
Whenever you want us.
We didn't like the things you said
The last time home.
Bourgeois, you said, and a word which sounded
Very like atrophied.
Daddy doesn't like the way you collect
Toilet graffiti,
God is dead – Nietzsche, and the reply,
Nietzsche is dead – God.

You can't expect Daddy to go round
With the plate in church
With thoughts like that in his head.
I worry too.
Structuralism sounds like a building-site,
Semiology sounds rather rude
In a medical kind of way.
The dogs are well, both almost human,
As we've often said
To you.

Please wear a vest, the days are getting
Colder. We hope you will not be so rude
The next time home.
Daddy and I have just re-done your room.
The blood on the wall hardly shows
After two coats of paint.
Cambridge must be very pretty just now.
I am, in spite of everything,
Your loving Mother.

Stretch Marks

Lying awake in a provincial town
I think about poets. They are mostly
men, or Irish, turn out old yellow
photographs, may use four letter words,
stick pigs or marry twice, and edit
most of the books and magazines.

Most poets, who are men, and get to
the bar first at poetry readings,
don't like us fey or even feminist,
too old, too young, or too intense,
and monthlies to them are just the
times when very few need us.

Gowned like women in funereal black
they have friends who went punting
on the Cam. I'm not too clear
what others did in Oxford, except
avoid the traffic, bathe in fountains,
drunkenly, a different shade of blue.

Mostly they teach, and some must be
fathers, but they have no stretch marks
on their smooth stomachs to prove it.
At least we know our children
are our own. They can never really
tell, but poems they can be sure of.

Mr Zwiegenthal

He was your other father, she said,
awkwardly. I was lucky to have
two fathers, I thought, but he was
a secret; left behind a bow-tie
like a black malevolent butterfly,
a looped violin string, an address
in Danzig, a baby in her bed.

Played beautiful he did, at the end
of the pier, the August sun dipping
slowly into the sea, the turnstile
creaking as they ran home, laughing,
sliding on shingle, clutching stones
and shells, but careful with his fiddle
and the black suit she used to mend.

What did he think, I asked, my real dad,
when he came home from India and found me
sleeping in the crib beside her?
Wasn't he pleased? Her face grew
cracked all over. The lodger, a Jew,
it wasn't meant... a mistake, the pills
didn't work. I felt so bad, so bad.

Mr Zwiegenthal, I have your nose,
your hands, but no talent for a waltz,
a barcarolle. I know you almost as well
as I know myself, with your dark moods,
and your tall stooping figure which broods
over my whole life, looking out across
the Baltic, and in your buttonhole a rose.

Themes for women

There is love to begin with, early love,
painful and unskilled, late love for matrons
who eye the beautiful buttocks and thick hair
of young men who do not even notice them.

Parturition, it figures, comes after, cataclysmic
at first, then dissolving into endless care
and rules and baths and orthodontic treatment,
Speech days, Open days, shut days, exams.

There are landscapes and inscapes too, sometimes tracts
of unknown counties, most often the one great hill
in low cloud, the waterfall, the empty sands, the few
snowdrops at the back door, the small birds flying.

Politics crop up at election time and ecology
any old time, no ocelot coats, no South African
oranges, a knowledge of the Serengeti
greater than the positioning of rubbish dumps
here in this off-shore island in hard times.

Seasons never go out of fashion, never will,
the coming of Spring, the dying fall
of Autumn into Winter, fine brash summers,
the red sun going down like a beach ball
into the sea. These do not escape the eyes
of women whose bodies obey the tides
and the cheese-paring sterile moon.

As you might expect, death hangs around a lot.
First ageing mothers, senile fathers; providing
the ham and sherry when the show is over,
examining stretched breasts to catch the process
of decay in time. In farmhouse kitchens they make
pigeon pies, weeping unexpectedly over
curved breasts among the floating feathers.
The men tread mud in after docking lambs' tails,
and smell of blood.

PATRICIA BEER

In Memory of Stevie Smith

A goodbye said after a party, after the drive home,
Is often final, to be labelled
Months later as the last word, meaninglessly.
The one who goes inside, clicking
The door after a polite pause, and the one who drives
Off still have something to discuss.

There had been friendship, not close, coming late in the day
With darkness already tropically near.
I remember an outing through the lanes near Hereford
With Easter weather and a fantastic
Story about gold plate in a stately home
That made us laugh till the car swerved.

Mrs Arbuthnot, Phoebe and Rose, must have died
Long ago, and Mrs Courtley
Though she had a few years of conversation left.
Mrs Arbuthnot we know became
A wave, a long and curling wave that broke
Upon a shore she had not expected.

Muriel, dressed up to the nines, with even
Her tiara on, must in the end
Have heard death knock, and opened to her beau
With the black suit come to take her out.
The swimmer whose behaviour was so misinterpreted
At last stopped both waving and drowning.

A heroine is someone who does what you cannot do
For yourself and so is this poet. She discovered
Marvels: a cat that sings, a corpse that comes in
Out of the rain. She struck compassion
In strange places: for ambassadors to hell, for smelly
Unbalanced river gods, for know-all men.

Return to Sedgemoor

'Battle of Sedgemoor. Come and bring your friends.'
And so they have I see. Dragging me down
Into this pageant of what was once real.
I died here but I cannot now recall
Which side I fought on. And until today –
Comfortable in warm weather hoping something,
Tetchy in winter dreading everything –
I've been content simply to know I was
Once here. How shocking the oblivion
Of coming back to sight and sound, to north
And south, to right and wrong, at a complete loss.

The cows are gazing at the popping cannon.
What roars they must have heard to go on chewing
At noise that shot the meat out of our mouths.
I seem to see the guns for the first time,
Plump little pigs. I hear a voice explaining
That they were known as 'Hot Lips' and 'Sweet Lips'.
I swear we never called them anything
Like that. I first made love on a battlefield,
I remember – though not which or who –
And realised there was a difference
Between love and war: I don't remember what.

Sedgemoor took place at night, and it's enough
To make a ghost laugh in the sun to see
These fluent creatures dash about regardless
While we, with elbows, knees and arse and chin
Stuck out at angles, had to feel our way.
These willow trees were low and strong to hang
Men in the morning light – as they are doing
Now – but in the dark they merely gave
Us bloody noses. Memory does not return
Like experience, more like imagination:
How it would have been if, how it must.

'The last battle to be fought on English soil'
The voice concludes. No riots, no pretenders
Or invaders in what must be years?

No, I am a ghost and do not wish
To understand the present. Let me
Concentrate on getting my life back.
My memory is like a severed muscle
And there's no friend or foe or animal
To recognise me. On the night I died
King's men and rebels all hastened away
As if some moon came up to light them home.

The Lost Woman

My mother went with no more warning
Than a bright voice and a bad pain.
Home from school on a June morning
And where the brook goes under the lane
I saw the back of a shocking white
Ambulance drawing away from the gate.

She never returned and I never saw
Her buried. So a romance began.
The ivy-mother turned into a tree
That still hops away like a rainbow down
The avenue as I approach.
My tendrils are the ones that clutch.

I made a life for her over the years.
Frustrated no more by a dull marriage
She ran a canteen through several wars.
The wit of a cliché-ridden village
She met her match at an extra-mural
Class and the OU summer school.

Many a hero in his time
And every poet has acquired
A lost woman to haunt the home,
To be compensated and desired,
Who will not alter, who will not grow,
A corpse they need never get to know.

She is nearly always benign. Her habit
Is not to stride at dead of night.
Soft and crepuscular in rabbit-
Light she comes out. Hear how they hate
Themselves for losing her as they did.
Her country is bland and she does not chide.

But my lost woman evermore snaps
From somewhere else: 'You did not love me.
I sacrificed too much perhaps,
I showed you the way to rise above me
And you took it. You are the ghost
With the bat-voice, my dear. *I* am not lost.'

Election Night

'Politicians are a race apart' says a fellow viewer
Far into election night. We have lost our sleep
With these strange people. The winners, like counting horses,
Have got it right and been led off home.

We see the losers, in a junket dawn,
Heading out of yesterday along the M4,
Overtaking frowsy trucks, driving at ninety,
Stopping on the hard shoulder to confer.

We see them again drawn up before their houses.
Flowers which are neighbourless and neglected
Straggle and gasp over synthetic urns.
The affronted cat holds its back legs stiff.

They are unreal, yet they haul their luggage
Out of the boot like anybody else returning.
We are aware of the contents: toothbrushes and pyjamas
Smelling seedily of gum and groin.

The show is over. Through the window in the stairs
We see the magpie, our own returning officer,
Land on the back field among the buttercups
That make a mayoral chain around his chest.

The Third Eyelid

Today the black cat has grown a third eyelid,
A white crescent coming in from the corner,
Overlaying the dark pupil. Her eternal stare
Is switched over to time now. Stress or disease
Has made a freak out of the trapeze artist.

And tonight there is an eclipse of the moon,
A black crescent on lightness. The print
And the negative look at each other
Across the valley, two moons, two cats,
Waiting to see which moves first.

It is a hallowe'en out of season.
Informally the souls whirl round the fields,
Tap on the cobbles, scrabble in the thatch.
In the house a radio chatters about death.
The evening air is cool with portents.

Goodbye to the round moon and the perfect eye
And tomorrow. Seventeen years old, the cat
Should be the first to crumble away
But the moon can no longer be counted on.
It may scatter before this poem is done.

A wide cloud with an edge as rough as soil
Rises to cover the eclipse. If the moon
Is spared it will draw a tide of earth
Up over the cat, the white sparkle in the corner
Of her shut eye, and her black lips.

CONNIE BENSLEY

Comfort

In a meadow, redolent of summer,
Deep in green, each leaf gilded
Against the sky, sit three women
Smiling at the camera. They are fat
Beyond the merely Rubenesque.

Corseted in folding chairs,
Armoured in synthetics;
Their considerable legs stretch forward in unison.
In the East, they would be collectors' pieces.

One has a striped umbrella
Over her head. She suffers with the sun.
Another has the thermos, which she's handing on to Flo,
For Flo gets parched; and all of them are kind.

Indeed, if you were lost – if you had missed the path
That led back round the hill
They'd help you; they would hem you in
And wall you round with helpfulness.

Such a stockade:
No harm could penetrate.
You'd be safe there,
Safe, and in clover.

Trespass

I turned to you,
Smelling out warmth like a cat,
Preying on you decorously
For touch and comfort.

We always want more than we bargain for –
The particular tone of voice,
The special intimacy,
The exclusive offer.

To appear in your mind's eye
Couched in glowing terms
And under your hand in dreams
Was my desire.

But reality was more of the commonplace.
I learned to stand in line for your largesse;
To ask for nothing, and to look for less.

Cookery

Strange how the heat both softens and hardens:
Turning sinews to gelatine
And liquid batters into crispness and substance
Or cricket-bat solidity.

Soon, I will take you and feed you
My stew. It will be thick, reddish brown,
And rich as the beginning of the world.
In it will be dark mouthfuls engorged with wine,
Crusted and melded with gold and amber tenderness.

Rumour of it will reach you from the kitchen,
Embarrassing you with saliva –
But when you eat, I shall leave the room,
For you must be alone to commune
With this dark tide, which will flood,
Like evangelism, through the blood
Under your pale accountant's skin.

Later, I will sit with you over crumbly meringues
And you will smile, under the pearls on your moustache.

Such goodness. I know it is right.
You will soften and harden for me.

Hyperosmia

Dread and some of the related emotions
will often reach me by way of the nose.
                    SAUL BELLOW
                    Henderson the Rain King

He, smelling of sandalwood aftershave;
mature but virginal; panicky:

she crying, pleading, casting off
discretion and clothing.

The memory terribly recalled to her
by a haunting of sandalwood.

You cannot always have what you want,
it taunts.

Much later, when the air has cleared,
Thank God, she replies.

Politeness

They walked awkwardly along the towpath
bumping together, because his arm
was round her shoulder. He was saying:
I shall always remember this walk.
I'll never forget last night.
I'll never forget you. Oh God.

After a pause, she made a short
non-committal noise. The morning had turned
wet and dark. She felt dilapidated by the rain
and of course had forgotten her umbrella
due to the unexpected turn of events.
Trust me, he said, *you will, won't you?*

Trust him to what, she wondered.
Which men could one trust? Any man
carrying a musical instrument, perhaps?
Any man walking along reading a book?
Most doctors – with reservations about those
wearing bow ties. *Trust you to what?* she asked.

To never let you down, he said,
splitting the infinitive, crushing her
against his wet tweeds. She fought
for breath as he loomed over her.
Little one, I can't let you go.
I'll be back on Thursday. Expect me.

So many imperatives. The situation
had become unwieldy. She longed
for buttered toast, looked furtively
at her watch. *I know, I know, we have
so little time.* The suffocating squeeze
into the spongy lapels.

I've never felt like this before
Have you ever felt like this before?
Fatigue and embarrassment were
all too familiar to her. She stirred the leaves
with the toe of her boot. *No* she said
politely. *Not exactly like this.*

SUJATA BHATT

શેરડી   (Shérdi)

The way I learned
to eat sugar cane in Sanosra:
I use my teeth
to tear the outer hard *chaal*
then, bite off strips
of the white fibrous heart –
suck hard with my teeth, press down
and the juice spills out.

January mornings
the farmer cuts tender green sugar-cane
and brings it to our door.
Afternoons, when the elders are asleep
we sneak outside carrying the long smooth stalks.
The sun warms us, the dogs yawn,
our teeth grow strong
our jaws are numb;
for hours we suck out the *russ*, the juice
                           sticky all over our hands.

So tonight
when you tell me to use my teeth,
to suck hard, harder,
then, I smell sugar cane grass
               in your hair
and imagine you'd like to be
shérdi   shérdi   out in the fields
        the stalks sway
               opening a path before us

શેરડી   (Shérdi): sugar cane.

What Is Worth Knowing?

That Van Gogh's ear, set free
wanted to meet the powerful nose
of Nevsky Avenue.
That Spain has decided to help
NATO. That Spring is supposed to begin
on the 21st of March.
That if you put too much salt in the *keema*
just add a few bananas.
That although the Dutch were the first
to help the people of Nicaragua they don't say much
about their history with Indonesia.
That Van Gogh collected Japanese prints.
That the Japanese considered
the Dutch to be red-haired barbarians.
That Van Gogh's ear remains full of questions
it wants to ask the nose of Nevsky Avenue.
That the vaccinations for cholera, typhoid and yellow fever
are no good – they must be improved.
That red, green and yellow are the most
auspicious colours.
That turmeric and chilli powder are good
disinfectants. Yellow and red.
That often Spring doesn't come
until May. But in some places
it's there in January.
That Van Gogh's ear left him because
it wanted to become a snail.
That east and west
meet only in the north and south – but never
in the east or west.
That in March 1986 Darwinism is being
reintroduced in American schools.
That there's a difference
between pigeons and doves, although
a ring-dove is a wood-pigeon.
That the most pleasant thing is to have a fever
of at least 101 – because then the dreams aren't
merely dreams but facts.

That during a fever the soul comes out
for fresh air, that during a fever the soul bothers to
speak to you.
That tigers are courageous and generous-hearted
and never attack unless provoked –
but leopards,
leopards are malicious and bad-tempered.
That buffaloes too,
water-buffaloes that is, have a short temper.
That a red sky at night is a good sign for sailors,
for sailors...what is worth knowing?
What is worth knowing?

Muliebrity

I have thought so much about the girl
who gathered cow-dung in a wide, round basket
along the main road passing by our house
and the Radhavallabh temple in Maninagar.
I have thought so much about the way she
moved her hands and her waist
and the smell of cow-dung and road-dust and wet canna lilies,
the smell of monkey breath and freshly washed clothes
and the dust from crows' wings which smells different –
and again the smell of cow-dung as the girl scoops
it up, all these smells surrounding me separately
and simultaneously – I have thought so much
but have been unwilling to use her for a metaphor,
for a nice image – but most of all unwilling
to forget her or to explain to anyone the greatness
and the power glistening through her cheekbones
each time she found a particularly promising
mound of dung –

White Asparagus

Who speaks of the strong currents
streaming through the legs, the breasts
of a pregnant woman
in her fourth month?

She's young, this is her first time,
she's slim and the nausea has gone.
Her belly's just starting to get rounder
her breasts itch all day,

and she's surprised that what she wants
is *him*
      inside her again.
Oh come like a horse, she wants to say,
move like a dog, a wolf,
                  become a suckling lion-cub –

Come here, and here, and here –
but swim fast and don't stop.

Who speaks of the green coconut uterus
the muscles sliding, a deeper undertow
and the green coconut milk that seals
her well, yet flows so she is wet
from his softest touch?

Who understands the logic
behind this desire?
Who speaks of the rushing tide
                  that awakens
her slowly increasing blood – ?
And the hunger
            raw obsessions beginning
with the shape of asparagus:
sun-deprived white and purple-shadow-veined,
she buys three kilos
of the fat ones, thicker than anyone's fingers,
she strokes the silky heads,
some are so jauntily capped...
            even the smell pulls her in –

EAVAN BOLAND

I Remember

I remember the way the big windows washed
out the room and the winter darks tinted
it and how, in the brute quiet and aftermath,
an eyebrow waited helplessly to be composed

from the palette with its scarabs of oil
colours gleaming through a dusk leaking from
the iron railings and the ruined evenings of
bombed-out, post-war London; how the easel was

mulberry wood and, porcupining in a jar,
the spines of my mother's portrait brushes
spiked from the dirty turpentine and the face
on the canvas was the scattered fractions

of the face which had come up the stairs
that morning and had taken up position in
the big drawing-room and had been still
and was now gone; and I remember, I remember

I was the interloper who knows both love and fear,
who comes near and draws back, who feels nothing
beyond the need to touch, to handle, to dismantle it,
the mystery; and how in the morning when I came down –

a nine-year-old in high, fawn socks –
the room had been shocked into a glacier
of cotton sheets thrown over the almond
and vanilla silk of the French Empire chairs.

An Irish Childhood in England: 1951

The bickering of vowels on the buses,
the clicking thumbs and the big hips of
the navy-skirted ticket collectors with
their crooked seams brought it home to me:
Exile. Ration-book pudding.
Bowls of dripping and the fixed smile
of the school pianist playing 'Iolanthe',
'Land of Hope and Glory' and 'John Peel'.

I didn't know what to hold, to keep.
At night, filled with some malaise
of love for what I'd never known I had,
I fell asleep and let the moment pass.
The passing moment has become a night
of clipped shadows, freshly painted houses,
the garden eddying in dark and heat,
my children half-awake, half-asleep.

Airless, humid dark. Leaf-noise
The stirrings of a garden before rain.
A hint of storm behind the risen moon.
We are what we have chosen. Did I choose to? –
in a strange city, in another country,
on nights in a north-facing bedroom,
waiting for the sleep that never did
restore me as I'd hoped to what I'd lost –

let the world I knew become the space
between the words that I had by heart
and all the other speech that always was
becoming the language of the country that
I came to in nineteen fifty-one:
barely-gelled, a freckled six-year-old,
overdressed and sick on the plane,
when all of England to an Irish child

was nothing more than what you'd lost and how:
was the teacher in the London convent who
when I produced 'I amn't' in the classroom
turned and said – 'you're not in Ireland now'.

The Muse Mother

My window pearls wet.
The bare rowan tree
berries rain.

I can see
from where I stand
a woman hunkering –
her busy hand
worrying a child's face,

working a nappy liner
over his sticky, loud
round of a mouth.

Her hand's a cloud
across his face,
making light and rain,
smiles and a frown,
a smile again.

She jockeys him to her hip,
pockets the nappy liner,
collars rain on her nape
and moves away,
but my mind stays fixed:

If I could only decline her –
lost noun
out of context,
stray figure of speech –
from this rainy street
again to her roots,
she might teach me
a new language:

to be a sibyl
able to sing the past
in pure syllables,
limning hymns sung
to belly wheat or a woman,

able to speak at last
my mother tongue.

C

Night Feed

This is dawn.
Believe me
This is your season, little daughter.
The moment daisies open,
The hour mercurial rainwater
Makes a mirror for sparrows.
It's time we drowned our sorrows.

I tiptoe in.
I lift you up
Wriggling
In your rosy, zipped sleeper.
Yes, this is the hour
For the early bird and me
When finder is keeper.

I crook the bottle.
How you suckle!
This is the best I can be,
Housewife
To this nursery
Where you hold on,
Dear life.

A silt of milk
The last suck.
And now your eyes are open,
Birth-coloured and offended.
Earth wakes.
You go back to sleep.
The feed is ended.

Worms turn
Stars go in.
Even the moon is losing face.
Poplars stilt for dawn
And we begin
The long fall from grace.
I tuck you in.

ALISON BRACKENBURY

Kingdoms

Gold, edged with green, the peacock's eyes
Ducked and shimmered past my head
To see the young Athenians
who could not leap the bull, lie dead.
Their ended screams still twist my sleep
become the staircase where I run,
of alabaster pale as milk
in courtyards where the black bull shone
his high horns lashed with reddened silk.

Black, pierced with grey, prick morning's leaves,
where all the headdresses lie dark
crushed in rough volcano ash;
where now we sleep in shelters, cracks
in painted stones: in fear I brush
for morning's sticks through the deep wood.

A young black bull they would have found
with net, gold rope for sacrifice
Stirs through the thicket: I am caught
only in his drowsing eyes:
a smudge of mist. He rubs the grey
smooth trunk; blinks sleep, walks slow away

For pomp and cold twigs crackle: fade.
In a still space I am drawn.
Fire, be moth-wing, grey and gold,
Bull and dancer: ash and dawn.

Black Dog

Cold broods over the house, like a white stare.
Across the lamps' lights, snow sprays feathers – stars –
You grind your blue shoes in my lap
All your new books are read.
                          But there are stories
Which drift, before we sleep, as far away
As lonely barns, from which the crumbled straw
Spills snow on frozen ground. Here is a story
Without a start or end, from the flat land
From which I came.
                          Now listen – You love dogs
The lumbering St Bernard, prancing Cairn –
A man is walking up a clouded lane
Head hot with drink; the night. What makes him turn?
High as the hedge, it stands. It watches him.
Its eyes are vast as stars.
                          On the low road
Skimming the dips, the new, fast cycle runs.
Why does the rider brake? He hears its breath, behind,
He races on; the blurring wheels gleam.
Harshly it blows, yet it lopes after him
Past every elm and gate, mile after mile.

Then, when he rushes in, no longer hot
With clear, scared eyes, they listen; then they nod.
Almost amused, they tell him, what he saw
Was the Black Dog.
                          It is seen everywhere:
But where I started, grew the calm idea
That under berried hedges, padding dark
It comes to keep you safe: to friend the night.

So much quick time lies wasted. So much fear –
Of wind, that cuts you, that could light you through,
Of quiet spiders spinning in the sun,
Of dark. There as he looked (though it was gone)
Over the plaited hawthorn reared the moon,
Lifted, through threads of cloud, a beating light.

You wriggle to the floor. Older than you
Stories do not stay still. They melt, like snow,
Trickle through books, to shine along my shelf.
In times of thaw, wandering indoors or out,
You may meet blacker dogs inside yourself.

Produce of Cyprus

Picking grapes from a paper bag, sucking the misted skin
I think of the island which grew them, Venus' ground
(the rain is in sheets on my window, wet, green, blind)
there, the dry song of the cicada, there the warm nights
with the window propped open, sea's stripe on the counterpane.

Yet they too, have their troubles. The frosts were late;
the land does not love us, relentless stony ground
though we own it down generations. The price of grapes
is falling; and so on. No doubt they dream of us
that far and prosperous country; on its window, the wealth of
          the rain.

The last is tough. The bag, as I put by the rest
rustles and whispers, Paradise is the place
of which we know nothing, which we know best.

Great Escapes

Myself, I honour Rachel, quick and dark,
As lovely as a gipsy; and as sharp.
She found a spacious Sunday morning weighed
By the straw-haired boy who had waylaid
Her on the school bus, daily. For a while
She walked by the closed stable, tried to smile,
Then told him 'Goodbye!' curtly and at once
Saddled the pony. With no backward glance

She rode off briskly to the wet, deep hills
Where tall blue cranesbill nods, raw whitethorn spills
Beside the gallop; while her sister, bent
By the fair boy and his fair-haired friend
Wondering which she should choose, stuffed lunch
Through wires at dozing rabbits in their hutch.

Rachel's thirteen, the pony, lent. Say then
That bolts to joy aren't possible again,
That – at thirty-three – all hopes are idle.
'Of course,' I murmur, buckling on the bridle.

JEAN 'BINTA' BREEZE

Spring Cleaning

de Lord is my shepherd
I shall not want

an she scraping
de las crumbs
aff de plate
knowing ants will feed

maketh me to lie down
in green pastures
leadeth me beside de still
waters

an she han washing clothes
spotless
lifting dem outa de water
drying she han careful slow
pon she apron

restoreth my soul

she mixing
sugar
water
lime
she filling she favourite jug
de one wid de cool palm pattern

yea though I walk
troo de valley of de
shadow of death

she opening de fridge
de cowl stapping her breath
for a motion

I will fear no evil

she put een wah she want
tek out wah she want
shut de door

for thou art wid me
thy rod an thy staff
dey comfort me

an she looking wid a far eye
pon de picture a de children
side a de almanac
pon de wall

surely goodness an mercy
shall follow me

she pick up de broom
an she sweeping

all de days of my life

an she sweeping

an I will dwell
in de house of de Lord

she sweeping out
sweeping
out

shake de broom
in de wind
dus fly
she beat it gains de fence
dus fly
she cup she han
unda de pipe
an she sprinkle water
roun she
stan up
hans akimbo

she watching
all de dark spirits
departing wid de dus

sunrise in er eyes

forever
an ever

For All Blue Notes

pull a blue note
from your sleeve
and wipe disaster
from your calling

hearing
the hereafter
light a brisk way
to desire

fly by right
to settle
daily discord

request a plant
that hums
and makes you grow

wouldn't you know
it could be far worse
getting better
holding on by
simply letting go
remembering to forget
all that you think you know

I Poet

ah was readin
readin all de time
fram book
fram play
fram t.v.
fram life
in odder words
fram yuh all
befo ah was writin
ah was readin
yuh all
neva did know who yuh all was but
ah was full a love
ah give it here
ah give it dere
neva see no harm
in a likkle share of
de warmes ting ah have
sista, bredda,
older, younger
neva matta
jus love
like evrybody was preachin
ah was readin
ah was lovin
befo ah was writin

ah read all yuh poems
ah read all yuh plays
ah read all tea leaf, palm,
anyting wid a good story
even if it didn't always have
a happy endin
an evryting ah read, ah sey,
but how come I know dis story aready? or
I do dat yesterday
I see dat last night
I live troo dat
so I stap readin fi a while

stap lovin fi a while
jus befo I start writin
I stap evryting
jus fi a moment
an I sey, maybe, (I humble)
I sey, maybe
it was you readin me all de time
so doah I was well hurt inside
wen yuh all did sey
I wasn't no poet
I never mind
cause I sey
I was poet all de time
so I start write
an I tankful
to madda an fadda
dat ah did read an love firs
fah I know
when I writin
I poem
is you
all you

HEATHER BUCK

The Poppy

The poppy cannot explain
The sun's turning away, cannot reproach
The sudden cold-shouldering,
After the warm fingering into the depths
Of its dark red centred self.

Meeting at Monemvassia

Inside your house a leafy court
where songbirds plucked their final frenzy
from withdrawing light, a darkened hall,
and silence like a great invasion from the sea,
peace that infiltrated, took you utterly.

You were wearing it that afternoon of heat
when cats stirred only for necessity,
as in the stillness it enfolded me.

Sitting on the wall you told me how a snake
lay coiled beside the church, how snakes
have always guarded treasure.
But in that atmosphere it seemed
that fighting dragons was some queer disease
born out of restlessness, born out of need
for anything that's absent, that is not now.

Was what we shared the treasure? That lack
of striving, that entire abandonment
to everything that is. So singular,
that even as I write I'm losing it
by wanting Monemvassia.

Lintel in the Museum at Nikopolis

Dorotheus and Marcella have erected it
to fulfil their promise – lst-2nd c. AD

Did they wreathe it with vines
and see the flagstones beneath
take on a patina of polish
from their own, and smaller
quick running feet, forcing
even the stones to acknowledge
their passage backwards and forwards,
in and out of the trauma of living?

And did they learn by sharing
each other, not to tip too much
of the discourse of self
in the spaces between, but leave
enough light and air to grow
like trees to shelter each other?

The Shattering

There is this hard shoulder
jutting into my life,
and the intolerable sea-thrust
that wears it away.

It seems that time doesn't vary
the incident, only darkens
and toughens the texture.
We are so vulnerable
we stand back
from the shattering.

But consent to stay
within its fragments, know
that at the hub of darkness
is this hollowed place
to cradle light.

Evening

Flushed dark as aubergine, the evening waits,
a hesitation in the day
when files and copy-books are packed away,
and girls in offices shake off
the tyranny of telephones,
for they inherit hours like rooms
which they inhabit and call their own.

The time when traffic swells and car doors slam,
as when a chapter springs to life,
the story moves, the idling mind
forgets the scuttle needing coal,
relaxes into bliss again.

When in an opened bottle wine
begins to seek its own decline,
and in a quickening of words
two lovers shed their separateness
and in each other lose themselves.

When through the railings of the park
the trees dissolve in smears of darkness,
and quizzing fingers of the wind,
like hands that ransack jumble,
frisk the pillowed leaves for tramps.

EILÉAN NÍ CHUILLEANÁIN

Swineherd

When all this is over, said the swineherd,
I mean to retire, where
Nobody will have heard about my special skills
And conversation is mainly about the weather.

I intend to learn how to make coffee, at least as well
As the Portuguese lay-sister in the kitchen
And polish the brass fenders every day.
I want to lie awake at night
Listening to cream crawling to the top of the jug
And the water lying soft in the cistern.

I want to see an orchard where the trees grow in straight lines
And the yellow fox finds shelter between the navy-blue trunks,
Where it gets dark early in summer
And the apple-blossom is allowed to wither on the bough.

The Second Voyage

Odysseus rested on his oar and saw
The ruffled foreheads of the waves
Crocodiling and mincing past: he rammed
The oar between their jaws and looked down
In the simmering sea where scribbles of weed defined
Uncertain depth, and the slim fishes progressed
In fatal formation, and thought

                              If there was a single
Streak of decency in these waves now they'd be ridged
Pocked and dented with the battering they've had,
And we could name them as Adam named the beasts,
Saluting a new one with dismay, or a notorious one
With admiration; they'd notice us passing
And rejoice at our shipwreck, but these
Have less character than sheep and need more patience.

I know what I'll do he said;
I'll park my ship in the crook of a long pier
(And I'll take you with me he said to the oar)
I'll face the rising ground and walk away
From tidal waters, up river-beds
Where herons parcel out the miles of stream,
Over gaps in the hills, through warm
Silent valleys, and when I meet a farmer
Bold enough to look me in the eye
With 'where are you off to with that long
Winnowing fan over your shoulder?'
There I will stand still
And I'll plant you for a gatepost or a hitching-post
And leave you as a tidemark. I can go back
And organise my house then.
                              But the profound
Unfenced valleys of the ocean still held him;
He had only the oar to make them keep their distance;
The sea was still frying under the ship's side.
He considered the water-lilies, and thought about fountains
Spraying as wide as willows in empty squares,
The sugarstick of water clattering into the kettle,
The flat lakes bisecting the rushes. He remembered spiders and
        frogs
Housekeeping at the roadside in brown trickles floored with mud,
Horse-troughs, the black canal, pale swans at dark:
His face grew damp with tears that tasted
Like his own sweat or the insults of the sea.

Letter to Pearse Hutchinson

I saw the islands in a ring all round me
And the twilight sea travelling past
Uneasy still. Lightning over Mount Gabriel:
At such a distance no sound of thunder.
The mackerel just taken
Battered the floor, and at my elbow
The waves disputed with the engine.
Equally grey, the headlands
Crept round the rim of the sea.

Going anywhere fast is a trap:
This water music ransacked my mind
And started it growing again in a new perspective
And like the sea that burrows and soaks
In the swamps and crevices beneath
Made a circle out of good and ill.

So I accepted all the sufferings of the poor,
The old maid and the old whore
And the bull trying to remember
What it was made him courageous
As life goes to ground in one of its caves,
And I accepted the way love
Poured down a cul-de-sac
Is never seen again.

There was plenty of time while the sea-water
Nosed across the ruinous ocean floor
Inquiring for the ruinous door of the womb
And found the soul of Vercingetorix
Cramped in a jamjar
Who was starved to death in a dry cistern
In Rome in 46 BC.

Do not expect to feel so free on land.

Deaths and Engines

We came down above the houses
In a stiff curve, and
At the edge of Paris airport
Saw an empty tunnel
– The back half of a plane, black
On the snow, nobody near it,
Tubular, burnt-out and frozen.

When we faced again
The snow-white runways in the dark
No sound came over
The loudspeakers, except the sighs
Of the lonely pilot.

The cold of metal wings is contagious:
Soon you will need wings of your own,
Cornered in the angle where
Time and life like a knife and fork
Cross, and the lifeline in your palm
Breaks, and the curve of an aeroplane's track
Meets the straight skyline.

The images of relief:
Hospital pyjamas, screens round a bed
A man with a bloody face
Sitting up in bed, conversing cheerfully
Through cut lips:
These will fail you some time.

You will find yourself alone
Accelerating down a blind
Alley, too late to stop
And know how light your death is;
You will be scattered like wreckage,
The pieces every one a different shape
Will spin and lodge in the hearts
Of all who love you.

Chrissie

Escaped beyond hope, she climbs now
Back over the ribs of the wrecked ship,
Kneels on the crushed afterdeck, between gross
Maternal coils: the scaffolding
Surviving after pillage.
                              On the strand
The voices buzz and sink; heads can be seen
Ducking into hutches, bent over boiling pans.
The trees above the sand, like guests,
Range themselves, flounced, attentive.
Four notches down the sky, the sun gores the planks;
Light fills the growing cavity
That swells her, that ripens to her ending.

The tide returning shocks the keel;
The timbers gape again, meeting the salty breeze;
She lies where the wind rips at her left ear,
Her skirt flapping, the anchor–fluke
Biting her spine; she hears
The dull sounds from the island change
To a shrill evening cry. In her head she can see them
Pushing out boats, Mother Superior's shoulder to the stern
(Her tanned forehead more dreadful now
Than when helmeted and veiled)
                              And she goes on fingering
In the shallow split in the wood
The grandmother's charm, a stone once shaped like a walnut,
They had never found. Salt water soaked its force:
The beat of the oars cancelled its landward grace.

She clings, as once to the horned altar beside the well.

GILLIAN CLARKE

The Water-Diviner

His fingers tell water like prayer.
He hears its voice in the silence
through fifty feet of rock
on an afternoon dumb with drought.

Under an old tin bath, a stone,
an upturned can, his copper pipe
glints with discovery. We dip our hose
deep into the dark, sucking its dryness,

till suddenly the water answers,
not the little sound we know,
but a thorough bass too deep
for the naked ear, shouts through the hose

a word we could not say, or spell, or remember,
something like 'dŵr...dŵr'.

Overheard in County Sligo

I married a man from County Roscommon
and I live at the back of beyond
with a field of cows and a yard of hens
and six white geese on the pond.

At my door's a square of yellow corn
caught up by its corners and shaken,
and the road runs down through the open gate
and freedom's there for the taking.

I had thought to work on the Abbey stage
or have my name in a book,
to see my thought on the printed page,
or still the crowd with a look.

But I turn to fold the breakfast cloth
and to polish the lustre and brass,
to order and dust the tumbled rooms
and find my face in the glass.

I ought to feel I'm a happy woman
for I lie in the lap of the land,
and I married a man from County Roscommon
and I live in the back of beyond.

Red Poppy

(from a painting by Georgia O'Keeffe)

'The meaning of a word
is not as exact
as the meaning of a colour'

So she walks out of the rectangles
of hard, crowded America
and floods the skies over southern plains

with carmine, scarlet,
with the swirl of poppy-silk.
There is music in it, and drumbeat.

You can put out the sun with poppy,
lie in long grass with beetle and ladybird
and shade your eyes with its awnings,

its heart of charcoal.
Wine glasses held to candles
or your veined lids against the sun.

The waters open for a million years,
petal after petal in the thundering river,
stamens of flying spray at its whirlpool heart.

Red mountain where the light slides
through the beating red of every Texan dusk,
and dark earth opens in a sooty yawn.

She paints out language, land, sky,
so we can only look and drown in deeps
of poppy under a thundering sun.

On Air

Tools of my father's art: old radios
of fretted wood and bakelite.
In a sanctum of shot-silk curtained window
crystal or valve lurked in its holy light.

I turned the knob. The needle wavered on
through crackling distances, Paris, Luxembourg, Hilversum,
past the call-sign of some distant station,
a lonely lightship where infinity scrambles to a hum

the Chinese whispers of a jabbering world.
And now, by transistor and satellite we hear
Beethoven in Berlin sooner than if we were there
on air-waves the speed of light. And when the wall crumbled

we heard the first stone fall before they could.
We watch storms darken the map from the crow's nest
of the weather satellite, hear the swallow's foot
on the wind's telegraph before she comes to rest,

the sun dried to a pellet in her throat.
Still lodged at the wingfeather's bloodroot
a grain of desert sand,
and on my car a veil of strange red dust.

Breakers Yard

Alsatians pick among the bones of Austins.
A mew of blind kittens in the dashboard
of a rusting Ford, butterflies shimmer
over ragwort and red valerian.

Metal and glass ring to the sound of hammers,
and fireweed burns
among miles of breakage,
old engines jammed in an August heatwave.

Bikes drop. We leave them spinning
to clamber the mudguards and bonnets
of old trucks and cars, leap from roof to roof,
stepping-stones too hot to stand on.

It sings like traffic crawling Brooklyn Bridge
in Saturday movies,
or humming the 8-lane freeways
of television.

I take the wheel of a grounded yellow Vauxhall
at the yard's bright heart
and burn headlong into the afternoon
till you scream for mercy.

Sometimes, driving the overpass,
I catch the eye of a mirror from the wreckers yard,
but never, now, a blue bicycle wheel,
its blurred spokes slowing.

WENDY COPE

Engineers' Corner

*Why isn't there an Engineers' Corner in Westminster
Abbey? In Britain we've always made more fuss of a
ballad than a blueprint...How many schoolchildren
dream of becoming great engineers?*

Advertisement placed in *The Times* by the Engineering Council

We make more fuss of ballads than of blueprints –
That's why so many poets end up rich,
While engineers scrape by in cheerless garrets.
Who needs a bridge or dam? Who needs a ditch?

Whereas the person who can write a sonnet
Has got it made. It's always been the way,
For everybody knows that we need poems
And everybody reads them every day.

Yes, life is hard if you choose engineering –
You're sure to need another job as well;
You'll have to plan your projects in the evenings
Instead of going out. It must be hell.

While well-heeled poets ride around in Daimlers,
You'll burn the midnight oil to earn a crust,
With no hope of a statue in the Abbey,
With no hope, even, of a modest bust.

No wonder small boys dream of writing couplets
And spurn the bike, the lorry and the train.
There's far too much encouragement for poets –
That's why this country's going down the drain.

Reading Scheme

Here is Peter. Here is Jane. They like fun.
Jane has a big doll. Peter has a ball.
Look, Jane, look! Look at the dog! See him run!

Here is Mummy. She has baked a bun.
Here is the milkman. He has come to call.
Here is Peter. Here is Jane. They like fun.

Go Peter! Go Jane! Come, milkman, come!
The milkman likes Mummy. She likes them all.
Look, Jane, look! Look at the dog! See him run!

Here are the curtains. They shut out the sun.
Let us peep! On tiptoe Jane! You are small!
Here is Peter. Here is Jane. They like fun.

I hear a car, Jane. The milkman looks glum.
Here is Daddy in his car. Daddy is tall.
Look, Jane, look! Look at the dog! See him run!

Daddy looks very cross. Has he a gun?
Up milkman! Up milkman! Over the wall!
Here is Peter. Here is Jane. They like fun.
Look, Jane, look! Look at the dog! See him run!

My Lover

For I will consider my lover, who shall remain nameless.
For at the age of 49 he can make the noise of five different kinds
　　　of lorry changing gear on a hill.
For he sometimes does this on the stairs at his place of work.
For he is embarrassed when people overhear him.
For he can also imitate at least three different kinds of train.
For these include the London tube train, the steam engine, and
　　　the Southern Rail electric.
For he supports Tottenham Hotspur with joyful and unswerving
　　　devotion.

For he abhors Arsenal, whose supporters are uncivilised and rough.
For he explains that Spurs are magic, whereas Arsenal are boring
        and defensive.
For I knew nothing of this six months ago, nor did I want to.
For now it all enchants me.
For this he performs in ten degrees.
For first he presents himself as a nice, serious, liberated person.
For secondly he sits through many lunches, discussing life and
        love and never mentioning football.
For thirdly he is careful not to reveal how much he dislikes losing
        an argument.
For fourthly he talks about the women in his past, acknowledging
        that some of it must have been his fault.
For fifthly he is so obviously reasonable that you are inclined to
        doubt this.
For sixthly he invites himself round for a drink one evening.
For seventhly you consume two bottles of wine between you.
For eighthly he stays the night.
For ninthly you cannot wait to see him again.
For tenthly this does not happen for several days.
For having achieved his object he turns again to his other interests.
For he will not miss his evening class or his choir practice for a
        woman.
For he is out nearly all the time.
For you cannot even get him on the telephone.
For he is the kind of man who has been driving women round the
        bend for generations.
For, sad to say, this thought does not bring you to your senses.
For he is charming.
For he is good with animals and children.
For his voice is both reassuring and sexy.
For he drives an A-registration Vauxhall Astra estate.
For he goes at 80 miles per hour on the motorways.
For when I plead with him he says, 'I'm not going any slower
        than *this*.'
For he is convinced he knows his way around better than anyone
        else on earth.
For he does not encourage suggestions from his passengers.
For if he ever got lost there would be hell to pay.
For he sometimes makes me sleep on the wrong side of my own
        bed.
For he cannot be bossed around.

For he has this grace, that he is happy to eat fish fingers or Chinese
      takeaway or to cook the supper himself.
For he knows about my cooking and is realistic.
For he makes me smooth cocoa with bubbles on the top.
For he drinks and smokes at least as much as I do.
For he is obsessed with sex.
For he would never say it is overrated.
For he grew up before the permissive society and remembers his
      adolescence.
For he does not insist it is healthy and natural, nor does he ask me
      what I would like him to do.
For he has a few ideas of his own.
For he has never been able to sleep much and talks with me late
      into the night.
For we wear each other out with our wakefulness.
For he makes me feel like a light-bulb that cannot switch itself off.
For he inspires poem after poem.
For he is clean and tidy but not too concerned with his appearance.
For he lets the barber cut his hair too short and goes round
      looking like a convict for a fortnight.
For when I ask if this necklace is all right he replies, 'Yes, if no
      means looking at three others.'
For he was shocked when younger team-mates began using talcum
      powder in the changing-room.
For his old-fashioned masculinity is the cause of continual
      merriment on my part.
For this puzzles him.

JENI COUZYN

The Beast

In our house he stalks silent
on padded feet. He has left
cracks on the floorboards, gouged
chasms in my father's face, ripped
bloody rivers across his eyes.
My mother believes she has
tamed him. Nights, she strokes his coarse
fur, coaxes him onto her
bed, his huge weight
rocks on her chest. Purring like thunder
shakes the curtains. In pitiful mucousy
scratching her breathing
aggravates the night. There are
bloodspots on her pillow. Hers.
He's been king in our house
for thirty years now. I told them
– Don't keep pets, they will
devour you. Leave them
roam the wide bush. He heard.
He knocked me to the ground
with a massive paw
flexed his claws on my back
licked the blood with his bone-cold
reptile tongue. I cowered on the floor
screaming. His great jaws
smiled over me, yellow black-flecked
teeth had bits of
raw meat in them. His breath came in hot
foul smelling waves. Don't
show fear, said my mother, he
likes you. – He
lives here, said my father, he's
one of us. You'll have to
get to know him. I saw his arm was
scarred with claw marks
wrist to shoulder.
– He's old, said my father, be
gentle with him.
You'll learn.

I Have Seen it Pulsing in your Veins

I have seen it pulsing in your veins
I have seen it silver all over your hair
and I've felt it perfectly
uncurl in my body
a new leaf uncurls in a room
a bright gull circling
hundreds of miles from the sea.
O mysteriously your skeleton
moves in your body
oceans of little fish lap and flow
in your limbs
and I have never seen you in the morning.

I have seen it in your hands
I have seen it glistening on your skin
I have felt it in my mind unfurling
have bitten into my flesh with pointed teeth
bitterly to control it and hold it in.

I have never seen your bones, nor will I
though they're eternal in you
like rocks and fossils
I have never seen a drop of your blood
nor do I know where you were born
yet I have seen it unfurl over your head
into the evening red with winter
and I've seen it taking root in the room
seeding and rooting in a celebration of green.

Soon it will begin again.
You will live on, and grow old, and your dear
body will bend and wrinkle. On your lips
made small and neat
many kisses hang, still unsung
words wait in your head like seeds
and footsteps
wait in your feet. You have planted your seed also
in the belly of your son and your daughter –
you're forever a garden

and though your absence
fills my house
I give you back the sun and the wide night now
my precious one.

Dawn

Of your hand I could say this
a bird poised mid-air in flight
as delicate and smooth.

Of your mouth
a foxglove in its taking
without edges or hurt.

This of your ear
a tiny sea-horse, immortal
sporting in white waves

and of your eye
a place where no one could hide
nothing lurk.

Of your cupped flesh
smooth in my palm
an agate on the sea-shore

of your back and belly
that they command kisses.
And of your feet I would say

they are inquisitive and gay
as squirrels or birds
and so return to your hand

and begin my voyage
around your loveliness
again and yet again

as in my arms you lie sleeping.

The Message

The message of the men is linear.
Like rapid pines they swarm upwards
jostling for space
mutilating their roots in the race
sowing a shade so deep
within their conquered space
little else can grow
and *growth*, they are shouting, *growth*.

But the message of the women is love
has always been love.
It is the luminous shining
under the substance
opaque stickiness of pain and grief
greyness of wanting, heaviness of getting.

The saints knew it also
the wisemen, the incarnations of God
Christ, Buddha
brought it as an astonishing revelation.

But we were born knowing it.
It is the circle of light we carry
at the centre of our bodies
knowing, and forgetting
see with our eyes in visionary radiance
when we give birth
and lose and discover again
season after season
because we are orchard.

HILARY DAVIES

The Ophthalmologist

We are in a very dark room.
He has the air of one not gone above
For years; his whisper shows
He is completely in command down here.
So I commend myself into his gentle fingers
That play around my head more intimately
Than most men's should do, the trembling
At my ear, the pressure on my temples,
Making me turn profile from side to side,
The touch testing my neck.
He has many categories of sight, ranged
In little boxes, a long, a short, an astigmatism
In a prism of glass. His machinery
Flickers an instant before me, lenses
You'd love to turn in your hand
Like ovals of limestone, waxy as opal.
All the kingdoms he shows me of letters
From their different angles: bold,
Crabbed, melancholic. I peer through
The thicknesses, pitting myself guiltily
Against deft fingers, the deferential mask.

Half an hour's enough to pinpoint all my weaknesses;
How to correct blur, squint, failure to see things
As they really are. I've grown to like
The shadowiness with which we work,
How outlines turn to sculpture, the world
Dividing into lamplight and the dark.
When he throws wide the door, I cannot rise
Towards the greening surface;
Under the desks and curtains the eye-doctor
Offers the lure of many visions,
The honey of his systems underground.

So I Climbed Out of the Hatch

So I climbed out of the hatch
Following the order that had come
From deep within the ship
To try the rigging. Began to step
Up and along the ropes, testing
And pulling my weight against the wind
Bitter and from the north. Salt
Flayed my eyes and hands till I
Could feel and see and think of
No more but the next strong twist
Of creosoted line my life was strung on.
But then came one from the belly
Of the ship behind me, with whom I'd
Eaten, drunk, and shared a bed,
Lifting his gentle eyes up.
Called encouragement against the tossing
And started out along the spar
As my safeguard, his voice as powerful
As the rope that bore us.
Yet I, too conscious of my weakness,
Clinging with all my sinew
To the cordage, moved on by inches
Not looking down nor up, but only
Concentrating on the texture of this
One grip, this moment in my hand.
And now I do not know how many years
Have slipped away since first I started
Up into the storm, but notice
How powerful I am become, and ruthless,
Finding myself wide out along this spar
And catching far far below me his desperate voice,
His dying gentle eyes.

The Mushroom Gatherer

When the summer visitors come out here
They first notice him at market
His oilcloth covered with horns of plenty,
Horse mushrooms, good-to-eat chanterelles.
'Buy for a soup pot, a stew, winter pickling
And salting'; his hands are filthy
As dead men's fingers, he lines his baskets with moss.
By noon he's around the outhouses
Asking for eggs and pullets; he mews
And smiles to cajole the women.
The visitors are sceptical when girls tell
How he dances in fairy rings, how his moustache
Is pale from drinking mushroom beer.
Yet every summer there's one who hitches up
Her skirt and goes with him under the broad-leaved trees
Which are the habitat of some, or among
Rotting branch heads, or dried dung.
They cut sticks and spend days in the forest,
Splaying freckled toes, feeling for mounds
That'll show them the dark convolutions of truffles.
When she returns, everyone's amazed at her sorting
Of baskets the greenhorns bring her,
Only the shade of a smile as she tosses out
He who is most handsome, the destroying angel,
Crafty cap, phallus impudicus.

Tattoo in the Convict Camp

At ten o'clock when the lights go down
And they know there'll be silence
Unless it's the dread expected, which is not to be
Thought of once between now and morning,
They turn to the little man cross-legged with his spine
Not fitting the wall and plead with him, 'Vlodya! Vlodya!
Show us the circus!' He laughs, and spits;

Touches their shoulders with the tips of his fingers
Before flicking open the buttons and belt and flies:
His bone-lean thighs are caparisoned horses
Leaping through hoops and back again;
Here shimmying up and down pectorals are the monkeys in fezes
Buttocks up to the audience and the pink tutus
Of the trapeze ballerinas bobbing right across
That diaphragm. Here are elephants
Docking their foreheads along a neural column:
They roll it like teak round and round their lips
Testing for flavour. And the lions on the biceps
Shake their manes and canines test for size
The head of the ringmaster popping out
Clean as a whistle to take his bow
From the spectators roaring now for the pièce
De résistance: cannon slowly tilting at the sky,
And a shiver going down them as their heads turn
Into the dome of the big top, hoping the shot
May go clear through the canvas and hit the immaculate stars.
They sigh 'Vlodya! Vlodya!' as he falls back sweating,
Is applauded and the spent circus animals rubbed down
To avoid the agues of fear and sequestration.
When they huddle back to cages, it's twenty degrees below.

NUALA NÍ DHOMHNAILL

Geasa

Má chuirim aon lámh ar an dtearmann beannaithe,
má thógaim droichead thar an abhainn,
gach a mbíonn tógtha isló ages na ceardaithe
bíonn sé leagtha ar maidin romham.

Tagann aníos an abhainn istoíche bád
is bean ina seasamh inti.
Tá coinneal ar lasadh ina súil is ina lámha.
Tá dhá mhaide rámha aici.

Tairrigíonn sí amach paca cártaí,
'An imréofá breith?' a deireann sí.
Imrímid is buann sí orm de shíor
is cuireann sí de cheist, de bhreith is de mhórualach orm

Gan an tarna béile a ithe in aon tigh,
ná an tarna oíche a chaitheamh faoi aon díon,
gan dhá shraic chodlata a dhéanamh ar aon leaba
go bhfaighead í. Nuair a fhiafraím di cá mbíonn sí,

'Dá mba siar é soir,' a deireann sí, 'dá mba soir é siar.'
Imíonn sí léi agus splancacha tintrí léi
is fágtar ansan mé ar an bport.
Tá an dá choinneal fós ar lasadh le mo thaobh.

D'fhág sí na maidí rámha agam.

The Bond

If I use my forbidden hand
To raise a bridge across the river,
All the work of the builders
Has been blown up by sunrise.

A boat comes up the river by night
With a woman standing in it,
Twin candles lit in her eyes
And two oars in her hands.

She unsheathes a pack of cards,
'Will you play forfeits?' she says.
We play and she beats me hands down,
And she puts three banns upon me:

Not to have two meals in one house,
Not to pass two nights under one roof,
Not to sleep twice with the same man
Until I find her. When I ask her address,

'If it were north I'd tell you south,
If it were east, west.' She hooks
Off in a flash of lightning, leaving me
Stranded on the bank,

My eyes full of candles,
And the two dead oars.

[translated from the Irish by Medbh McGuckian]

Mo Theaghlach

Ag seo agaibh, go hachomair, mo theaghlach
an teaghlach a d'fhág meidhreach mo chroí.
Ins an seomra suite tá mo dheirfiúr Aoife
ar a corraghiob ag bailiú pinginí
a thit laistiar den dtolg is den bpianó
rianta deireanacha a spré a chuaigh amú,
deir sí an fáth go bhfuil sé ag imeacht i mbóiléagar
ná an rud a bhailíodar de dhroim an diabhail
gur faoina bholg arís a imíonn sé, airiú.

Ins an seomra folcaidh tá m'uncail Dónall
ag dul faoi loch sa dabhach mar fhomhuiréan.
Is dóigh leis má choimeádann sé a cheann síos
ná tabharfaimid faoi ndeara é a bheith ann.
Táimse mór leis is tuigim an stair atá laistiar de
an fáth gur fuath leis caint, cadráil nó biadán,
is nuair a théim thar bráid, tugaim trí rap ar an ndoras
ag fógrú dó go bhfuil aige *All-Clear*.

Ins an dtolglann níl aon tine ins an ngráta
ach é tógtha suas ó bhonn ag crann mór groí
atá préamhaithe i lúidín clé mo dhearthár
is a fhásann aníos tré dhíon is tré fhraitheacha an tí.
Deirtear go b'ann a chuir cailín éigin mallacht air
de bhrí gur dhein sé éigean uirthi bliain
leadránach éigin thiar ins na caogadaí.
Ní stopann sé ach ag slogadh *aspirin* leis an bpian.

Sa seomra leapan taobh thiar den leaba dhúbailte
tá cófra mór agus doras uaithne air.
Laistiar de tá dhá leanbh ar bheagán meabhrach
ná tagann amach riamh faoin ngaoth nó faoin ngrian.
Tá siad á gcoimeád ann ar chuma na *Hairy Babies*
a mhair áit éigin thuaidh in aice le Trá Lí.
N'fheadar éinne againn i gceart cé hí a máthair
is tá náire orainn go léir gur saolaíodh iad.

Household

My household. This is the shape of it, more or less,
The ways it has of gladdening my heart:
Look in the living-room, there's my sister Eva
Down on her hunkers picking up the pennies
That fell down behind the sofa and the piano –
The last scraps of her fortune she went through.
She says the reason it flew so fast
Is, what you get off the devil's back you lose
Under his belly, more's the pity.

Try the bathroom. My Uncle Donal
Submerges like a U-boat in the tub.
He thinks if he keeps his head under water
We'll never notice that he's there.
I get on with him, I know the whole story,
And why he is afraid of gossip and talk.
I give three raps on the door when I go past –
A signal between us to give him the *All-Clear*.

In the parlour the grate is empty,
The whole room is taken up with a great tree
Its root spreading from under my brother's left toenail,
Branches growing up through the roof and the rafters.
It's supposed to be a curse a girl put on him
When he laid heavy hands on her one time
Donkeys years ago, back in the fifties.
He's forever eating aspirins with the pain.

In behind the big bed in the master bedroom
There's a hidden press with a door painted green.
Behind the door two half-witted children
Never come out, rain or shine.
They're kept in there just like the Hairy Babies
That used to live up north beside Tralee.
None of us rightly knows who the mother is;
We are all of us ashamed they were ever born.

Thíos sa siléar a gheofá an file filiúil
col ceathar dúinn atá leochaileach, feosaí.
Bhíodh sé de shíor is choíche ag cumadh píosaí filíochta
is ár mbodhradh leo go dtí gur chuireamair gobán ar a bhéal.
Fuadaíodh é is cuireadh ceangal na gcúig gcaol air
is ar chuma éigin bíonn sé chomh mallaithe leis an ndiabhal
uair 'má seach go n-éiríonn leis teacht aníos chughainn
ba dhóigh leat go raibh adharca air is é ag tarrac slabhraí ina dhiaidh.

Sa seomra rúnda a chíonn sibh i mbarr an staighre
tá seanbhean a bhíonn de shíor ag eascainí.
Ní thógann éinne aon cheann a thuilleadh dá healaí
go háirithe nuair a éilíonn sí gurb í Caitlín Ní Uallacháin í.
Bhuaileas-sa léi lá is gan í ródhona
is dúirt sí liom gurb é a hainm ceart ná Grace Poole.
N'fheadarsa ó thalamh Dé cé bhí i gceist aici
is fiú dá mbeadh a fhios fhéin ar Éirinn ní neosfainn cé hí.

Amuigh ar an ndíon, ins an seanchás tae is both dó
tá seanduine leis féin i bhfolach ón slua.
Caitheann tú dul thar dhroichead clár chun teacht air
is ní maith leis daoine a chuireann air aon dua.
Tá sé ráite go maireann sé go sona sásta
le *harem* breis is trí fichid leannán sí.
Tá sé ráite gur dhúnmharaigh sé mo mháthair.
Tá sé ráite gurb é m'athair críonna é.

Down in the cellar you'll meet the bardic poet,
A first cousin that was always bad with his nerves.
He was forever coming out with bits of rhymes
And he'd deafen us with them till we put the muzzle on him.
We had him put in a strait waistcoat –
He's as cross as the devil anyway;
If he manages an odd time to climb the stairs
You'd swear you saw something with horns, dragging a chain.

In that secret room you see at the top of the stairs
There's an old one that's never done cursing.
Nobody pays any notice, especially not
When she screams that she is Caitlín Ní hUalláchain.
I met her one time on one of her good days
And she told me her real name was Grace Poole.
I haven't the least idea what she was talking about,
And if I had – I dare not breathe her name.

Out on the roof living in a tea-chest
There is an old man alone keeping out of trouble.
You have to cross the plank bridge to find him
And he isn't fond of people who come asking questions.
The story goes that he lives like a pasha
Up there with a couple of dozen succubi;
The story goes that he murdered my mother.
The story they tell is that he is my grandfather.

[translated from the Irish by Eiléan Ní Chuilleanáin]

MAURA DOOLEY

Drought

In the fiercest summer for years
gouts of sun sour milk in an hour,
rubbish simmers in streets which
steam with piss, swimming pools
pulse like tins of maggots
and all the time your postcards come.

Every village green turns brown,
reservoirs crack and rivers shrivel.
Each time I try to picture your face
sweat breaks over me
sudden as a storm
and all the time your postcards come.

Views of the Seine, the Tiber, the Nile,
necks of gondolas hooking through mist,
the Rhône, the Ganges, the Orinoco,
diving for danger at Acapulco.
All I ask's a screw, the shrink, a drink.
Honey, why do I always dream of death?

I can never slake this thirst,
can't eat, can't sleep, can't work, can't breathe,
my skin is scorched: the earth is tinder,
for nights I watch the hillside burn,
sparks hanging in the dark, like stars
and all the time your postcards come.

Heat silts up every artery,
the passages to my brain run dry.
Light thickens, clots, there is no shade.
Hair on my arms is bleached to straw.
You could put a match to me
but all the time, your postcards come.

Mansize

Now you aren't here I find
myself ironing linen squares,
three by three, the way
my mother's always done,
the steel tip steaming over your
blue initial. I, who resent
the very thought of this back-breaking
ritual, preferring radiator-dried
cottons, stiff as boards, any amount
of crease and crumple to this
soothing, time-snatching, chore.

I never understood my father's trick,
his spare for emergencies, but was glad
of its airing-cupboard comforts often enough:
burying my nose in it, drying my eyes
with it, staunching my blood with it,
stuffing my mouth with it. His expedience,
my mother's weekly art, leaves me
forever flawed: rushing into newsagents
for Kleenex, rifling your pockets in the cinema,
falling on those cheap printed florals,

when what I really want is Irish linen,
shaken out for me to sink my face in,
the shape and scent of you still warm
in it, your monogram in chainstitch
at the corner. Comforter, seducer, key witness
to it all, my neatly folded talisman,
my sweet flag of surrender.

Apple Pie in Pizzaland

We are apologising to one another
for our shynesses. The waitress apologises
for the lack of sultanas (not like the picture,
she says). I still probe between the slices of
apple as if I expect to find something other than
air. You spin the menu and pleat the paper napkin,
our cutlery scrapes eloquently enough.

On the train here a Canadian told me how
his province holds a lake the size of England.
I imagine you and I and Pizzaland, the green tables,
Doncaster, the fields, motorways, castles and flats,
churches, factories, corner shops, pylons, Hinkley Point,
Lands End and all of us dropped
in that huge lake, *plop*.

Years later new people will stroll on
the banks, remarking how in drought
you might see the top of Centrepoint
and in the strange stillness hear the ghostly
ring and clatter of Pizzaland forks on plates.

Does It Go Like This?

The day seawater swilled my lungs
he guided me back without ever once touching me.
Lying on shingle, like the two halves
of the equator, I thought my heart would burst,

not knowing in which element it drowned.
Now, two hundred miles from him, beached
on larkspur, lark song, I struggle to remember
something I used to know: *did it go like this? Like that?*

How did it start? At Capel-y-Ffin what rises
from dark red dirt, what's netted now is Heartsease,
flotsam of sheep skull filleted by lice,
a dead pony's ribs taut as ship's rigging

and here, where a draught of summer
rinses tired skin with cuckoo syncopation,
with percussion of bees, old fears rush in
fierce as a tide, blood, not birdsong

pulses at my ear: the strong cross-currents
that beat in these shallows, the meat
and bone under bright meadow grasses,
the heart's tricky business of staying alive.

Remember the day we saw divers trawl the Thames
heavy with rosaries of gas and rope,
angels with black rubber wings and serious faces
dropping through mist and into the deep, like psalms?

What is that tune whose words I try to catch
Does it go like this? Like this? How does it begin?
I dredge up only the middle, a jaded chorus,
of a song I used to know right through by heart.

The Celestial Announcer

On the day that you hear
the station announcer
call out the towns and villages
of your life, as if she'd read
the very chapters of your soul,
that knowing way she has of saying *Halifax*,
the way she skirts around poor rainy *Manchester*,
and jumps to the conclusion now of *Luddenden*
– with its ghost of a station
and dream of Branwell drunk under the stars –
and all the big and little places
you have ever been, would like to go,
chanted, charted;
well, then you realise it's time to change
your mind, ticket, journey,
point of departure,
Estimated Time of Arrival
and know that she will lend you wings
for those golden slippers, milk and honey,
bread, roses and a brand new map.

FREDA DOWNIE

Her Garden

My grandmother grew tiny grapes and tiger-lilies,
But there is no sentimental cut to her garden
Through a fat album or remembered lane;
Only interior voyages made on London ferries

Paddling the Thames' wicked brew to Silvertown,
Where regular as boot boys, the factories
Blacked her house every day, obscured the skies
And the town's sweet name at the railway station.

Between ships parked at the end of the road
And factory gates, she kept her home against soot,
Kept her garden colours in spite of it –
Five square feet of bitterness in a paved yard

Turned to the silent flowering of her will,
Loaded with dusty beauty and natural odours,
Cinnamon lilies, and the vine roots hanging grapes,
Sour as social justice, on the wash-house wall.

Railway Butterfly

Early sun rivets you to the station wall
And flattens your colours on the platform,
But should you desire anything at all
Beyond the warmth of this gritty place,
You will learn honey is never shunted here.

Perhaps you are that thoughtful gentleman
With more than time enough to spare
Dreaming he is, without doubt, a butterfly;
In which case, this dry suspension
Will be acceptable enough.

But, if you are that frail proposition
Dreaming you are a philosopher,
Then, like me, you cannot be unaware
Of aridity's interminable dimensions
Entering the questionable dream we share.

Mountain Road

I contract to a heart beat.
It is not a swung lantern suddenly explaining
The shape of black trees, but the summer moon.

It is an absurd size,
Swollen with light and floating out of orbit,
Capable of eclipsing the entire night.
It is not a disc to reckon with, a nursery moon
Drawn or pasted at a reasonable distance.
The old man has gone and only mountains remain,
Ranged impersonal heaps shadowing moon and earth.

Unable to match thought with this immensity,
My feet flounder on the earth's steep sides

And scuttling, I descend
To a different prospect of twilight sea
Where a dreary light flattens the water's rim,
Hopeless as the framed gloom of a sleepless night.
The shore rocks are black as death, are meaningless,
And livid clouds narrowing the light
Hang level with me, weathered to a vision
Of enormous hands, supernatural and waiting.

The grey grass at my feet
Smells sweeter than it did at noon, but I want
A room of easy dimensions and words to answer.

Moon

Let alone the moon
Preserving her pocked face.
I have been over familiar
With her pitiless stare and know
She uses arsenic to whiten her hands.

How she eats my flesh.
How she disregards my bones
While bleaching them.

Gloves

Descending the gloom of early stairs,
I find someone has left
A small complex sculpture in the hall –
Until I see more clearly
It is your gloves lying there,
Fat-fingered, enormous; like gloves
Waiting for a ball-game to commence.

Thinking of your finely cast hands,
I see them quite deliberately
Dropping their tailored impedimenta
Before driving cold morning air.

Yet, settled as bronze,
The gloves' fingers stay curled.
They do not lose their grip.

CAROL ANN DUFFY

Standing Female Nude

Six hours like this for a few francs.
Belly nipple arse in the window light,
he drains the colour from me. Further to the right,
Madame. And do try to be still.
I shall be represented analytically and hung
in great museums. The bourgeoisie will coo
at such an image of a river-whore. They call it Art.

Maybe. He is concerned with volume, space.
I with the next meal. You're getting thin,
Madame, this is not good. My breasts hang
slightly low, the studio is cold. In the tea-leaves
I can see the Queen of England gazing
on my shape. Magnificent, she murmurs
moving on. It makes me laugh. His name

is Georges. They tell me he's a genius.
There are times he does not concentrate
and stiffens for my warmth. Men think of their mothers.
He possesses me on canvas as he dips the brush
repeatedly into the paint. Little man,
you've not the money for the arts I sell.
Both poor, we make our living how we can.

I ask him Why do you do this? Because
I have to. There's no choice. Don't talk.
My smile confuses him. These artists
take themselves too seriously. At night I fill myself
with wine and dance around the bars. When it's finished
he shows me proudly, lights a cigarette. I say
Twelve francs and get my shawl. It does not look like me.

Warming Her Pearls

Next to my own skin, her pearls. My mistress
bids me wear them, warm them, until evening
when I'll brush her hair. At six, I place them
round her cool, white throat. All day I think of her,

resting in the Yellow Room, contemplating silk
or taffeta, which gown tonight? She fans herself
whilst I work willingly, my slow heat entering
each pearl. Slack on my neck, her rope.

She's beautiful. I dream about her
in my attic bed; picture her dancing
with tall men, puzzled by my faint, persistent scent
beneath her French perfume, her milky stones.

I dust her shoulders with a rabbit's foot,
watch the soft blush seep through her skin
like an indolent sigh. In her looking-glass
my red lips part as though I want to speak.

Full moon. Her carriage brings her home. I see
her every movement in my head...Undressing,
taking off her jewels, her slim hand reaching
for the case, slipping naked into bed, the way

she always does...And I lie here awake,
knowing the pearls are cooling even now
in the room where my mistress sleeps. All night
I feel their absence and I burn.

Translating the English, 1989

...and much of the poetry, alas, is lost in translation...

Welcome to my country! We have here Edwina Currie
and The Sun newspaper. Much excitement.
Also the weather has been most improving
even in February. Daffodils. (Wordsworth. Up North.) If you like
Shakespeare or even Opera we have too the Black Market.
For two hundred quids we are talking Les Miserables,
nods being as good as winks. Don't eat the eggs.
Wheel-clamp. Dogs. Vagrants. A tour of our wonderful
capital city is not to be missed. The Fergie,
The Princess Di and the football hooligan, truly you will
like it here, Squire. Also we can be talking crack, smack
and Carling Black Label if we are so inclined. Don't
drink the H₂0. All very proud we now have
a green Prime Minister. What colour yours? Binbags.
You will be knowing of Charles Dickens and Terry Wogan
and Scotland. All this can be arranged for cash no questions.
Ireland not on. Fish and chips and the Official Secrets Act
second to none. Here we go. We are liking
a smashing good time like estate agents and Neighbours,
also Brookside for we are allowed four Channels.
How many you have? Last night of Proms. Andrew
Lloyd-Webber. Jeffrey Archer. Plenty culture you will be agreeing.
Also history and buildings. The Houses of Lords. Docklands.
Many thrills and high interest rates for own good. Muggers.
Much lead in petrol. Filth. Rule Britannia and child abuse.
Electronic tagging, Boss, ten pints and plenty rape. Queen Mum.
Channel Tunnel. You get here fast no problem to my country
my country my country welcome welcome welcome.

Valentine

Not a red rose or a satin heart.

I give you an onion.
It is a moon wrapped in brown paper.
It promises light
like the careful undressing of love.

Here.
It will blind you with tears
like a lover.
It will make your reflection
a wobbling photo of grief.

I am trying to be truthful.

Not a cute card or a kissogram.

I give you an onion.
Its fierce kiss will stay on your lips,
possessive and faithful
as we are,
for as long as we are.

Take it.
Its platinum loops shrink to a wedding-ring,
if you like.
Lethal.
Its scent will cling to your fingers,
cling to your knife.

Litany

The soundtrack then was a litany – *candlewick*
bedspread three piece suite display cabinet –
and stiff-haired wives balanced their red smiles,
passing the catalogue. *Pyrex.* A tiny ladder
ran up Mrs Barr's American Tan leg, sly
like a rumour. Language embarrassed them.

The terrible marriages crackled, cellophane
round polyester shirts, and then The Lounge
would seem to bristle with eyes, hard
as the bright stones in engagement rings,
and sharp hands poised over biscuits as a word
was spelled out. An embarrassing word, broken

to bits, which tensed the air like an accident.
This was the code I learnt at my mother's knee, pretending
to read, where no one had cancer, or sex, or debts,
and certainly not leukaemia, which no one could spell.
The year a mass grave of wasps bobbed in a jam-jar;
a butterfly stammered itself in my curious hands.

A boy in the playground, I said, *told me*
to fuck off; and a thrilled, malicious pause
salted my tongue like an imminent storm. Then
uproar. *I'm sorry, Mrs Barr, Mrs Hunt, Mrs Emery,*
sorry, Mrs Raine. Yes, I can summon their names.
My mother's mute shame. The taste of soap.

HELEN DUNMORE

Privacy of rain

Rain. A plump splash
on tense, bare skin.
Rain. All the May leaves
run upward, shaking.

Rain. A first touch
at the nape of the neck.
Sharp drops kick the dust, white
downpours shudder
like curtains, rinsing
tight hairdos to innocence.

I love the privacy of rain,
the way it makes things happen
on verandahs, under canopies
or in the shelter of trees
as a door slams and a girl runs out
into the black-wet leaves.
By the brick wall an iris
sucks up the rain
like intricate food, its tongue
sherbetty, furred.

Rain. All the May leaves
run upward, shaking.
On the street bud-silt
covers the windscreens.

Safe period

Your dry voice from the centre of the bed
asks 'Is it safe?'

and I answer for the days as if I owned them.
Practised at counting, I rock
the two halves of the month like a cradle.

The days slip over their stile
and expect nothing. They are just days,

and we're at it again, thwarting
souls from the bodies they crave.

They'd love to get into this room
under the yellow counterpane
we've torn to make a child's cuddly,

they'd love to slide into the sheets
between soft, much-washed
flannelette fleece,

they'd love to be here in the moulded spaces
between us, where there is no room,

but we don't let them. They fly about gustily,
noisy as our own children.

A cow here in the June meadow

A cow here in the June meadow
where clouds pile, tower above tower.

We lie, buried in sunburn,
our picnic a warm
paper of street tastes,

she like a gold cloud
steps, moony.
Her silky rump dips
into the grasses, buffeting
a mass of seed ready to run off in flower.

We stroll under the elder, smell
wine, trace blackfly along its leaf-veins

then burning and yawning we pile
kisses onto the hot upholstery.

Now evening shivers along the water surface.
The cow, suddenly planted, stands – her tender
skin pollened all over –
ready to nudge all night at the cold grasses,
her udder heavily and more heavily swinging.

Wild strawberries

What I get I bring home to you:
a dark handful, sweet-edged,
dissolving in one mouthful.

I bother to bring them for you
though they're so quickly over,
pulpless, sliding to juice,

a grainy rub on the tongue
and the taste's gone. If you remember
we were in the woods at wild strawberry time

and I was making a basket of dockleaves
to hold what you'd picked,
but the cold leaves unplaited themselves

and slid apart, and again unplaited themselves
until I gave up and ate wild strawberries
out of your hands for sweetness.

I lipped at your palm –
the little salt edge there,
the tang of money you'd handled.

As we stayed in the wood, hidden,
we heard the sound system below us
calling the winners at Chepstow,
faint as the breeze turned.

The sun came out on us, the shade blotches
went hazel: we heard names
bubble like stock-doves over the woods

as jockeys in stained silks gentled
those sweat-dark, shuddering horses
down to the walk.

Three Ways of Recovering a Body

By chance I was alone in my bed the morning
I woke to find my body had gone.
It had been coming. I'd cut off my hair in sections
so each of you would have something to remember,
then my nails worked loose from their beds
of oystery flesh. Who was it got them?
One night I slipped out of my skin. It lolloped
hooked to my heels, hurting. I had to spray on
more scent so you could find me in the dark,
I was going so fast. One of you begged for my ears
because you could hear the sea in them.

First I planned to steal myself back. I was a mist
on thighs, belly and hips. I'd slept with so many men.
I was with you in the ash-haunted stations of Poland,
I was with you on that grey plaza in Berlin
while you wolfed three doughnuts without stopping,
thinking yourself alone. Soon I recovered my lips
by waiting behind the mirror while you shaved.
You pouted. I peeled away kisses like wax
no longer warm to the touch. Then I flew off.

Next I decided to become a virgin. Without a body
it was easy to make up a new story. In seven years
every invisible cell would be renewed
and none of them would have touched any of you.
I went to a cold lake, to a grey-lichened island,
I was gold in the wallet of the water.
I was know to the inhabitants, who were in love
with the coveted whisper of my virginity:
all too soon they were bringing me coffee and perfume,
cash under stones. I could really do something for them.

Thirdly I tried marriage to a good husband
who knew my past but forgave it. I believed in the power
of his penis to smoke out all those men
so that bit by bit my body service would resume,
although for a while I'd be the one woman in the world
who was only present in the smile of her vagina.
He stroked the air where I might have been.
I turned to the mirror and saw mist gather
as if someone lived in the glass. Recovering
I breathed to myself, '*Hold on! I'm coming.*'

JEAN EARLE

Jugged Hare

She mourned the long-ears
Hung in the pantry, his shot fur
Softly dishevelled. She smoothed that,
Before gutting – yet she would rather
Sicken herself, than cheat my father
Of his jugged hare.

A tender lady, freakish as the creature –
But resolute. She peeled it to its tail.
Oh, fortitude! Her rings sparked in and out
Of newspaper wipes. Blood in a bowl,
Sacrificial gravy. A rarely afforded
Bottle of port.

She sustained marriage
On high events, as a child plays house.
Dramas, conciliations –
Today, the hare. She sent me out
To bury the skin,
Tossed the heart to the cat.

She was in full spate.

Fragrance of wine and herbs
Blessed our kitchen; like the hare's dessert
Of wild thyme; or like his thighs
As though braised by God. She smiled
And dished up on willow,
Having a nice touch in framing
One-off scenarios.

After the feast, my father was a lover
Deeply enhanced.
I heard them go to bed,
Kissing – still inside her picture.
Later, I heard her sob
And guessed it was the hare

Troubled her. My father slept,
Stunned with tribute. She lay now
Outside her frame, in the hare's dark

Hating her marital skills
And her lady-hands, that could flense a hare
Because she wooed a man.
In years to come,
I understood.

Young Girls Running

Almost, flight...

Herons, angling
A tilted grace. Spring twigs,
Taking the awkward wind.

Three-as-one, linked onrush
Mirrored in polished sand,
Light legs
Spattering pools, shells.

'The sea!' they cry, 'the sea!'
Birdlike, birdshape

Breasting the tide
With no breasts, merged
In the thrown wave

Which will rain them
Rosy, swept
Through its firming sting,
Medicinal shock, thrust...

They will be women,
Breasted, hipped,
Salted,
When they come out.

Menopause

Now and again –
Since I was quite young –
I reckon my quota of seed
That we stopped from growing: not, of course,
All would have made it – there wasn't time
Nor strength in myself. But I think of them.

We raised three – and couldn't really have done
With more. It just feels strange
I might have had a dozen
Persons in my gift: and who would they have been?

In school biology, we were told once
How the female seeds
Are laid down at her making; one to go
Every month, when her body's ready,
Taking its chance.

I remember sniggers – also, myself
Looking from the window
Even as I smirked. What a day it was,
Blue and white...
And the thing seemed wonderful?

Seed by seed, lined up for years,
Waiting in my dark for the blind push
To be someone. More curious to me
Than the well-known puzzles,
Everyone's go. God – the stars...

I don't suppose Jack ever gave a thought
To such ideas. Men are so wasteful,
Careless of their seed. I often guess
What lives those might have had
Given some luck.

The colours of their eyes...

To Father and Mother

When you return in dreams,
You smile, you are never cross with each other.
On the bizarre picnic, the fall-away cliff,
We dream together.

Often the fogs of war
Clogged my young breath, often you stood
Like two lighthouses, stabbing your powerful beams
Crosswise above my head.

You always smiled at me,
Never guessing at my built-in radar –
Hear beyond hearing, say nothing, think huge
(Children, the world over).

Your parent joy in me
Was not enough; I wanted you to smile so
One to the other – partners and relaxed,
As in finding mushrooms.

Now, in dreams, you do.

U.A. FANTHORPE

Not My Best Side

(Uccello: S. George and the Dragon, The National Gallery)

I

Not my best side, I'm afraid.
The artist didn't give me a chance to
Pose properly, and as you can see,
Poor chap, he had this obsession with
Triangles, so he left off two of my
Feet. I didn't comment at the time
(What, after all, are two feet
To a monster?) but afterwards
I was sorry for the bad publicity.
Why, I said to myself, should my conqueror
Be so ostentatiously beardless, and ride
A horse with a deformed neck and square hoofs?
Why should my victim be so
Unattractive as to be inedible,
And why should she have me literally
On a string? I don't mind dying
Ritually, since I always rise again,
But I should have liked a little more blood
To show they were taking me seriously.

II

It's hard for a girl to be sure if
She wants to be rescued. I mean, I quite
Took to the dragon. It's nice to be
Liked, if you know what I mean. He was
So nicely physical, with his claws
And lovely green skin, and that sexy tail,
And the way he looked at me,
He made me feel he was all ready to
Eat me. And any girl enjoys that.
So when this boy turned up, wearing machinery,
On a really *dangerous* horse, to be honest,
I didn't much fancy him. I mean,
What was he like underneath the hardware?

He might have acne, blackheads or even
Bad breath for all I could tell, but the dragon –
Well, you could see all his equipment
At a glance. Still, what could I do?
The dragon got himself beaten by the boy,
And a girl's got to think of her future.

III

I have diplomas in Dragon
Management and Virgin Reclamation.
My horse is the latest model, with
Automatic transmission and built-in
Obsolescence. My spear is custom-built,
And my prototype armour
Still on the secret list. You can't
Do better than me at the moment.
I'm qualified and equipped to the
Eyebrow. So why be difficult?
Don't you want to be killed and/or rescued
In the most contemporary way? Don't
You want to carry out the roles
That sociology and myth have designed for you?
Don't you realise that, by being choosy,
You are endangering job-prospects
In the spear- and horse-building industries?
What, in any case, does it matter what
You want? You're in my way.

FROM Stations Underground

1 *Fanfare*

*(for Winifrid Fanthorpe, born 5 February 1895,
died 13 November 1978)*

You, in the old photographs, are always
The one with the melancholy half-smile, the one
Who couldn't quite relax into the joke.

My extrovert dog of a father,
With his ragtime blazer and his swimming togs
Tucked like a swiss roll under his arm,
Strides in his youth towards us down some esplanade,

Happy as Larry. You, on his other arm,
Are anxious about the weather forecast,
His overdraft, or early closing day.

You were good at predicting failure: marriages
Turned out wrong because you said they would.
You knew the rotations of armistice and war,
Watched politicians' fates with gloomy approval.

All your life you lived in a minefield,
And were pleased, in a quiet way, when mines
Exploded. You never actually said
I told you so, but we could tell you meant it.

Crisis was your element. You kept your funny stories
Your music-hall songs for doodlebug and blitz-nights.
In the next cubicle, after a car-crash, I heard you
Amusing the nurses with your trench wit through the blood.

Magic alerted you. Green, knives and ladders
Will always scare me through your tabus.
Your nightmare was Christmas; so much organised
Compulsory whoopee to be got through.

You always had some stratagem for making
Happiness keep its distance. Disaster
Was what you planned for. You always
Had hoarded loaves or candles up your sleeve.

Houses crumbled around your ears, taps leaked,
Electric light bulbs went out all over England,
Because for you homes were only provisional,
Bivouacs on the stony mountain of living.

You were best at friendship with chars, gypsies,
Or very far-off foreigners. Well-meaning neighbours
Were dangerous because they lived near.

E

Me too you managed best at a distance. On the landline
From your dugout to mine, your nightly
Pass, friend was really often quite jovial.

You were the lonely figure in the doorway
Waving goodbye in the cold, going back to a sink-full
Of crockery dirtied by those you loved. We
Left you behind to deal with our crusts and gristle.

I know why you chose now to die. You foresaw
Us approaching the Delectable Mountains,
And didn't feel up to all the cheers and mafficking.

But how, dearest, will even you retain your
Special brand of hard-bitten stoicism
Among the halleluyas of the triumphant dead?

5 Sisyphus

> *The struggle itself towards the heights is enough to fill
> a man's heart. One must imagine Sisyphus happy.*
> CAMUS
> The Myth of Sisyphus

Apparently I rank as one
Of the more noteworthy sights down here.
As to that, I can't judge, having
No time to spare for tourists.

My preoccupations are this stone
And this hill. I have to push
The one up the other.

A trivial task for a team, an engine,
A pair of horses. The interest lies
Not in the difficulty of the doing,

But the difficulty for the doer. I accept this
As my vocation: to do what I cannot do.
The stone and I are

Close. I know its every wart, its ribby ridges,
Its snags, its lips. And the stone knows me,
Cheek, chin and shoulders, elbow, groin, shin, toe,
Muscle, bone, cartilage and muddied skinprint,
My surfaces, my angles and my levers.

The hill I know by heart too,
Have studied incline, foothold, grain,
With watchmaker's patience.

Concentration is mutual. The hill
Is hostile to the stone and me.
The stone resents me and the hill.

But I am the mover. I cannot afford
To spend energy on emotion. I push
The stone up the hill. At the top

It falls, and I pursue it,
To heave it up again. Time not spent
On doing this is squandered time.

The gods must have had a reason
For setting me this task. I have forgotten it,
And I do not care.

The Poet's Companion

Must be in mint condition, not disposed
To hayfever, headaches, hangovers, hysteria, these being
The Poet's prerogative.

Typing and shorthand desirable. Ability
To function on long walks and in fast trains an advantage.
Must be visible/invisible

At the drop of a dactyl. Should be either
A mobile dictionary, thesaurus and encyclopaedia,
Or have instant access to same.

Cordon bleu and accountancy skills essential,
Also cooking of figures and instant recall of names
Of once-met strangers.

Should keep a good address book. In public will lead
The laughter, applause, the unbearably moving silence.
Must sustain with grace

The role of Muse, with even more grace the existence
Of another eight or so, also camera's curious peeping
When the Poet is reading a particularly

Randy poem about her, or (worse) about someone else.
Ability to endure reproaches for forgetfulness, lack of interest,
Heart, is looked for,

Also instant invention of convincing excuses for what the Poet
Does not want to do, and long-term ability to remember
Precise detail of each.

Must be personable, not beautiful. The Poet
Is not expected to waste time supervising
The Companion. She will bear

Charming, enchanted children, all of them
Variations on the Poet theme, and
Impossibly gifted.

Must travel well, be fluent in the more aesthetic
European languages; must be a Finder
Of nasty scraps of paper

And the miscellany of junk the Poet loses
And needs *this minute, now*. Must be well-read,
Well-earthed, well able

To forget her childhood's grand trajectory,
And sustain with undiminished poise
That saddest dedication: *lastly my wife,*

Who did the typing.

VICKI FEAVER

Crab apple jelly

Every year you said it wasn't worth the trouble –
you'd better things to do with your time –
and it made you furious when the jars
were sold at the church fête
for less than the cost of the sugar.

And every year you drove into the lanes
around Calverton to search
for the wild trees whose apples
looked as red and as sweet as cherries,
and tasted sharper than gooseberries.

You cooked them in the wide copper pan
Grandma brought with her from Wigan,
smashing them against the sides
with a long wooden spoon to split
the skins, straining the pulp

through an old muslin nappy.
It hung for days, tied with string
to the kitchen steps, dripping
into a bowl on the floor –
brown-stained, horrible,

a head in a bag, a pouch
of sourness, of all that went wrong
in that house of women. The last drops
you wrung out with your hands;
then, closing doors and windows

to shut out the clamouring wasps,
you boiled up the juice with sugar,
dribbling the syrup onto a cold plate
until it set to a glaze,
filling the heated jars.

When they were cool
you held one up to the light
to see if the jelly had cleared.
Oh, Mummy, it was as clear and shining
as stained glass and the colour of fire.

The crack

cut right through the house —
a thick wiggly line
you could poke a finger into,
a deep gash seeping
fine black dust.

It didn't appear overnight.
For a long time
it was such a fine line
we went up and down stairs
oblivious of the stresses

that were splitting
our walls and ceilings apart.
And even when it thickened
and darkened, we went on
not seeing, or seeing

but believing the crack
would heal itself,
if dry earth was to blame,
a winter of rain
would seal its edges.

You didn't tell me
that you heard at night
its faint stirrings
like something alive.
And I didn't tell you —

until the crack
had opened so wide
that if we'd moved in our sleep
to reach for each other
we'd have fallen through.

Marigolds

Not the flowers men give women –
delicately-scented freesias,
stiff red roses, carnations
the shades of bridesmaids' dresses,
almost sapless flowers,
drying and fading – but flowers
that wilt as soon as their stems
are cut, leaves blackening
as if blighted by the enzymes
in our breath, rotting to a slime
we have to scour from the rims
of vases; flowers that burst
from tight, explosive buds, rayed
like the sun, that lit the path
up the Thracian mountain, that we wound
into our hair, stamped on
in ecstatic dance, that remind us
we are killers, can tear the heads
off men's shoulders;
flowers we still bring
secretly and shamefully
into the house, stroking
our arms and breasts and legs
with their hot orange fringes,
the smell of arousal.

Judith

Wondering how a good woman can murder
I enter the tent of Holofernes,
holding in one hand his long oiled hair
and in the other, raised above
his sleeping, wine-flushed face,
his falchion with its unsheathed
curved blade. And I feel a rush
of tenderness, a longing
to put down my weapon, to lie
sheltered and safe in a warrior's
fumy sweat, under the emerald stars
of his purple and gold canopy,
to melt like a sweet on his tongue
to nothing. And I remember the glare
of the barley field; my husband
pushing away the sponge I pressed
to his burning head; the stubble
puncturing my feet as I ran,
flinging myself on a body
that was already cooling
and stiffening; and the nights
when I lay on the roof – my emptiness
like the emptiness of a temple
with the doors kicked in; and the mornings
when I rolled in the ash of the fire
just to be touched and dirtied
by something. And I bring my blade
down on his neck – and it's easy,
like slicing through fish.
And I bring it down again,
cleaving the bone.

ELAINE FEINSTEIN

Regret

Do not look backward, children.
A sticky burning sea still lies below.
The harsh air stings like sand

and here among these salty pillars
the unforgiving stand. Take
the mountain ledge, even though

it crumbles into dust. Walk or crawl,
you must let the rocks cut into your feet without pity.
And forget the smoking city. God punishes regret.

Rose

Your pantry stocked with sweet cooked fish,
    pink herring, Polish cucumbers
in newspaper, and on the gas
    a bristly hen still boiling into soup:
most gentle sloven, how I honour now
    all your enormous, unfastidious welcome.

And when the string of two brown carrier bags
    bit into your short fat fingers
you only muttered, doesn't matter
    doesn't matter. I didn't understand
why you continued living with a man
    who could not forgive you, could not

forgive your worst offence:
    your happiness in little.
Even a string of shells would give you pleasure,
    but we did not bring gifts often;
and now it is too late to thank you for
    the warmth of your wide bosom, and the dimpled arms
waiting to hug my own bewildered children.

Urban Lyric

The gaunt lady of the service wash
stands on the threshold and blinks in the sunlight.

Her face is yellow in its frizz of hair
and yet she smiles as if she were fortunate.

She listens to the hum of cars passing
as if she were on a country lane in summer,

or as if the tall trees edging this
busy street scattered blessings on her.

Last month they cut a cancer out of her throat.
This morning she tastes sunshine in the dusty air.

And she is made alert to the day's beauty,
as if her terror had wakened poetry.

Getting Older

The first surprise: I like it.
Whatever happens now, some things
that used to terrify have not:

I didn't die young, for instance. Or lose
my only love. My three children
never had to run away from anyone.

Don't tell me this gratitude is complacent.
We all approach the edge of the same blackness
which for me is silent.

Knowing as much sharpens
my delight in January freesia,
hot coffee, winter sunlight. So we say

as we lie close on some gentle occasion:
every day won from such
darkness is a celebration.

Muse
(for E.T.)

'Write something every day,' she said,
'even if it's only a line,
it will protect you.'

How should this be?
Poetry opens no cell,
heals no hurt body,

brings back no lover,
altogether, poetry is
powerless as grass.

How then should it defend us?
unless by strengthening
our fierce and obstinate centres.

Hayfever

When Timothy grass and Rye pollen flew
each year, I began to honk like a goose.

It was always summer and party time
for kissing and rolling in the grass

so I couldn't bear to stay at home in bed.
I painted my face with beige pancake

put drops in my eyes, and learnt instead
as my membranes flared and I gasped for air

how to feel out of things
even when there.

ELIZABETH GARRETT

Two Floras
(after Botticelli and Titian)

What if these two should meet –
After hours, on naked feet,
Their artless déshabillé
Turning no heads, no Roman eyes –
In some corridor of the Uffizi?

The one, with the chest of a child,
Dancing from her millefiori
Grove, light as a spore
On the wind, spilling
Flowers on the polished floor;

The other, loosening her shift
Irrevocably so she slips from her frame,
One breast exposed, slow, in her soft
Mass of flesh, cupping
The incidental rose.

And what if they should? –
There would be little to say
With only the language of flowers:
But differences, in the shrewd, mute way
Of women, would be observed.

The one, troubled by the other's lack
Of scent, the absence of her shadow,
The flowers of make-believe
That blossom from her lap
Where no men go;

The other, meeting gravity for the first time,
Checked in her weightless dance,
Senses power in the flesh's substance,
Its smell – of more than flowers –
And the coloured shadow it casts.

Oak Bride

Let earth be my pillow, and the bridal
Sheet be spread beneath this window
Where the moon rocks in its oak cradle.
And I shall sleepwalk down
The centuries until my dream grows
Rootwise; by morning I will know
How many miles four hundred years
Of water must be drawn.

All night the prodigal moon shook florins
On my bedspread. I knew then
I was a well of wishing, and all
Of me was water to be hauled.
The pull of a tree drinking is a kiss
Where darkness marries silence: by osmosis
I entered my dream. What is
Desire but reciprocal thirst?

Down centuries of drought, like a river
I softened the bed of my oak-dark lover
Till dawn broke where the great delta
Cast its branches to the sky.
Arms wide, mouth quick with desire,
Drinking my own reflection, I
Rooted there, palms cupping
The first drops like acorns falling.

Mother, Baby, Lover
(for Vanessa)

When in the darkness
Behind closed lids I perceive
The blind, furled fist
And the questing
Mouth, hungry as a kiss
For the place
Where she alone exists –

I think with infinite compassion
Of all the breast-
Starved lovers of our world undressing
You to drink at this
Soft inverted cup of maternal bliss
In gratitude, and less
Than ignorance of what they miss.

Double

Darling – I am not what I appear:
Single-hearted with my long brown hair
Plaited for safe-keeping.

Something I have undone –
A stray wisp, a random
Provocation – say, a grass clipping –

Has set my brown mane wild,
Casting oats in our careful field
While both our hands were sleeping.

This is no dream. Double I see
And am, courting duplicity
Like the suave surface of a stream

Flowing in two directions.
Am I the warped reflection,
The undertow, or the still scene

That witnesses its distortion,
Loving no less the portions
Of its selfhood that remain?

I am none and all.
The body in its close thrall,
The deceiving eye and mind.

I am my mother's daughter.
Cover my face with my hands,
My hands with water.

PAMELA GILLILAN

Doorsteps

Cutting bread brings her hands back to me –
the left, with its thick wedding ring,
steadying the loaf. Small plump hands
before age shirred and speckled them.

She would slice not downwards but across
with an unserrated ivory-handled carving knife
bought from a shop in the Edgware Road,
an Aladdin's cave of cast-offs from good houses –
earls and countesses were hinted at.

She used it to pare to an elegant thinness.
First she smoothed already-softened butter
on the upturned face of the loaf. Always white,
Coburg shape. Finely rimmed with crust the soft
halfmoon half-slices came to the tea table
herringboned across a doylied plate.

I saw away at stoneground wholemeal.
Each slice falling forward into the crumbs
to be spread with butter's counterfeit
is as thick as three of hers. Doorsteps
she'd have called them. And those were white
in our street, rubbed with hearthstone
so that they glared in the sun
like new-dried tennis shoes.

Home is the Hunter

She's watched for his return
at each day's evening, his briefcase
stuffed as if with deermeat,
umbrella a spent spear.

Forty years of triumphal entrances,
attentive welcomings, end in this
gift-loaded euphoric homecoming.
Something near to fear

stirs in her. The house
has been hers throughout the core
of every day, close shelter
for her busy morning hours,
her re-creative afternoons.
Now it opens its traitor door,
switches allegiance to his clamour,
his masterfulness, his more

insistent needs. How long had she
dug, hoed and planted the suburban
flower-patch, made it colourful
and fragrant for his weekend
leisure? Now he comes in with the air
of a pioneer, as if her patient garden
were wilderness for his first
cultivation; and she'll pretend

(habits are hard to break) when called on
to admire, that everything he grows
is magical, as if no million years
but he alone made this summer's rose.

Four Years

The smell of him went soon
From all his shirts.
I sent them for jumble,
And the sweaters and suits.
The shoes
Held more of him; he was printed
Into his shoes. I did not burn
Or throw or give them away.
Time has denatured them now.

Nothing left.
There will never be
A hair of his in a comb.
But I want to believe
That in the shifting housedust
Minute presences still drift:
An eyelash,
A hard crescent cut from a fingernail,
That sometimes
Between the folds of a curtain
Or the covers of a book
I touch
A flake of his skin.

Leviathan

You can't make whales
make whales.
Chickens don't seem to mind
laying eggs for you;
the patient cow
conceives at the squirt of a syringe;
shoals of fry
will populate concrete ponds –
but whales cannot be handled
contained
farmed
made familiar like dolphins or lions
herded like pigs or sheep.
Their procreation is their own affair
their milk for their own young.
Only in death does man
find them valuable.

None left alive,
their monumental bones
will stand stripped in museums,
their pictures wonderful on the page
at W in a child's alphabet,
like D for dodo
H for humanity.

LAVINIA GREENLAW

Boris Goes Fishing
(for Bill Swainson)

In my classroom Russia you commented on the weather,
said goodbye to Mother and goodbye to Father,
while I struggled with the tenses
that would let you spend the day by the lake.
Your journey was uneventful. You did not
get lost in a forest, follow strange music
and wander off a path that never saw daylight
to be seduced by a snow queen and rescued by wolves.
I couldn't even send you to Samarkand
to save a princess from being boiled in oil.

You were allowed a blue sky and a friendly dog,
when what you really wanted was a tidal wave
that would empty the Baltic into your basket.
The day passed quietly. You caught three fish
and I managed to get the dog to fall into the water.
At home that evening, Father commented on the weather
while Mother cooked the fish. They could have been
sturgeon travelled north from the Caspian Sea,
pregnant with caviar, flavoured with bison's grass
and served in a blaze of vodka, but I did not

go into detail. Boris, you were a nice boy,
but my hand was more used to carving a desk
than filling a notebook with cramped Cyrillics.
I was fourteen and knew the Russia of storybooks;
I didn't want to make space for the wild grammar,
soft adjectives, accusatives and instrumentals
that would take you there. Instead, you went
to bed at eight o'clock. Mother tucked you up and
commented on the weather. I could not pronounce 'revolution',
so I shut you in a drawer and went dancing.

Electricity

The night you called to tell me
that the unevenness between the days
is as simple as meeting or not meeting,
I was thinking about electricity –
how at no point on a circuit
can power diminish or accumulate,
how you also need a lack of balance
for energy to be released. *Trust it.*
Once, being held like that,
no edge, no end and no beginning,
I could not tell our actions apart:
if it was you who lifted my head to the light,
if it was I who said how much I wanted
to look at your face. *Your beautiful face.*

Love from a Foreign City

Dearest, the cockroaches are having babies.
One fell from the ceiling into my gin
with no ill effects. Mother has been.
I showed her the bitemarks on the cot
and she gave me the name of her rat-catcher.
He was so impressed by the hole in her u-bend,
he took it home for his personal museum.
I cannot sleep. They are digging up children
on Hackney Marshes. The papers say
when that girl tried to scream for help,
the man cut her tongue out. Not far from here.
There have been more firebombs,
but only at dawn and out in the suburbs.
And a mortar attack. We heard it from the flat,
a thud like someone dropping a table.
They say the pond life coming out of the taps
is completely harmless. A law has been passed
on dangerous dogs: muzzles, tattoos, castration.

When the labrador over the road jumped up
to say hello to Billie, he wet himself.
The shops in North End Road are all closing.
You can't get your shoes mended anywhere.
The one-way system keeps changing direction,
I get lost a hundred yards from home.
There are parts of the new *A to Z* marked simply
'under development'. Even street names
have been demolished. There is typhoid in Finchley.
Mother has brought me a lavender tree.

The Innocence of Radium

With a head full of Swiss clockmakers,
she took a job at a New Jersey factory
painting luminous numbers, copying the style
believed to be found in the candlelit backrooms
of snowbound alpine villages.

Holding each clockface to the light,
she would catch a glimpse of the chemist
as he measured and checked. He was old enough,
had a kind face and a foreign name
she never dared to pronounce: Sochocky.

For a joke she painted her teeth and nails,
jumped out on the other girls walking home.
In bed that night she laughed out loud
and stroked herself with ten green fingertips.
Unable to sleep, the chemist traced each number

on the face he had stolen from the factory floor.
He liked the curve of her eights;
the way she raised the wet brush to her lips
and, with a delicate purse of her mouth,
smoothed the bristle to a perfect tip.

Over the years he watched her grow dull.
The doctors gave up, removed half her jaw,
and blamed syphilis when her thighbone snapped
as she struggled up a flight of steps.
Diagnosing infidelity, the chemist pronounced

the innocence of radium, a kind of radiance
that could not be held by the body of a woman,
only caught between her teeth. He was proud
of his paint and made public speeches
on how it could be used by artists to convey

the quality of moonlight. Sochocky displayed
these shining landscapes on his walls;
his faith sustained alone in a room
full of warm skies that broke up the dark
and drained his blood of its colour.

His dangerous bones could not keep their secret.
Laid out for X-ray, before a single button was pressed,
they exposed the plate and pictured themselves
as a ghost, not a skeleton, a photograph
he was unable to stop being developed and fixed.

RITA ANN HIGGINS

The German for Stomach
(for Eva)

I was waiting for the twenty-past
in the rain, trying to think
of the German for stomach.

While I was racking
I took time out for
a stew fantasy.
When a blue Merc pulled
out in front of a brown Mini,
I had stew fantasy interruptus.

The man in the brown Mini
was blue and furious
but he didn't let on.
Poor Rex later that day.

The blue Merc made me think
of blue skies and blue seas,
then it came to me,
Bauch, that's it, *der Bauch*.
I said it to myself all the way home
except when I passed the graveyard,
time for another stew fantasy.

I got off near Kane's butchers.
Inside they were discussing
the gimp and colour of Sean Sweeney's
duodenum when the doctor opened him.
They called it the Northern Province.

It was on the tip of my tongue
and out it tumbled,
'*Bauch* is the German for stomach.'

His wife said,
'Are you sure you don't want
a carrier bag for that, loveen?'

I could see that
the butcher was overwhelmed,
he wanted to shout
'Lapis Lazuli, Lapis Lazuli,'
but instead he said,

'You wouldn't put a dog out in it.'

The Did-You-Come-Yets of the Western World

When he says to you:
You look so beautiful
you smell so nice –
how I've missed you –
and did you come yet?

It means nothing,
and he is smaller,
than a mouse's fart.

Don't listen to him...
Go to Annaghdown Pier
with your father's rod.
Don't necessarily hold out
for the biggest one;
oftentimes the biggest ones
are the smallest in the end.

Bring them all home,
but not together.
One by one is the trick;
avoid red herrings and scandal.

Maybe you could take two
on the shortest day of the year.
Time is the cheater here
not you, so don't worry.

Many will bite the usual bait:
They will talk their slippery way
through fine clothes and expensive perfume,
fishing up your independence.

These are,
The did-you-come-yets of the western world,
the feather and fin rufflers.
Pity for them they have no wisdom.

Others will bite at any bait.
Maggot, suspender, or dead worm.
Throw them to the sharks.

In time one will crawl
out from under thigh-land.
Although drowning he will say,

'Woman I am terrified, why is the house shaking?'

And you'll know he's the one.

The Deserter

He couldn't wait
just up and died
on me.

Two hours
two hours
I spent ironing
them shirts
and he didn't even
give me the pleasure
of dirtying them,

that's the type
of person he was,
would rather die
than please you.

But in his favour
I will say this for him,
he made a lovely corpse.
Looked better dead
than he did in our front room
before the telly,

right cock-of-the-walk
in that coffin
head slightly tilted back
like he was going to say
'My dear people'.

He couldn't wait
never,
like the time
before the All-Ireland
we were going to Mass,

he had to have a pint
or he'd have the gawks, he said
that's the type he was
talk dirty in front of any woman.

No stopping him
when he got that ulcer out,
but where did it get him,

wax-faced above
in the morgue
that's where.

He's not giving
out to me now
for using Jeyes Fluid
on the kitchen floor,

or stuffing the cushions
with his jaded socks...
and what jaded them?
Pub crawling jaded them,
that's what.

He's tightlipped now
about my toe separators,
before this
he would threaten them
on the hot ash.

The next time
I spend two hours
ironing shirts for him
he'll wear them.

SELIMA HILL

Elegy for the Bee-god

Stingless bees
were bred in tree hollows
for beeswax and honey.
Every year, in the month
called Tzec, the bee-keepers
played their raspadores
and danced across the fields
with bells and ribbons
round their feet, to honour
the fat bee-god, who buzzed
in the heated air
to their music.
He lived in a gold house
in the hotlands, and drank
cocoa sweetened with honey.

All's quiet now, it's June,
and he's not here, the late,
the long-forgotten bee-god,
who sped on zig-zag wings
across the sky to the faithful.
Cross-eyed, bejewelled
and tattooed, drumming
his fluffy yellow feet
on the tree hollows,
he gave the bees new hope,
and cocoa sweetened with honey.

If ever I find him – thin,
justly offended, dead
in the dry chaparral –
I will put jade beads
and honey on his tongue,
and wrap him in a shroud
of wings, and loop his neck
with pearls from Guatemala;

I will light him candles
of beeswax, bringing sleep,
and he will rest in the shade
of the First Tree,
and wait for me there –
humming a tune, and drinking
cocoa sweetened with honey.

The Unsuccessful Wedding-Night

It's all because of Buster.
Of course, it's unreasonable,
he couldn't possibly have come –
his barking, his midnight walk,
the way he scratches at the blankets –

but as she presses her face
into the pillow of the small hotel,
she can't help missing him
terribly. She imagines the two of them
hiking in bright sunshine

over the Western Ghats; and soon
she begins to whimper to herself,
her runny nose trailing
over the foam pillows
like the Vasco da Gama of snails.

Desire's a Desire

It taunts me
like the muzzle of a gun;
it sinks into my soul like chilled honey
packed into the depths of treacherous wounds;
it wraps me up in cold green sheets
like Indian squaws

who wrap their babies in the soft green sheathes of irises
that smell of starch;
it tattooes my shins;
it itches my thighs
like rampant vaginal flora;
it tickles my cheeks
like silkworms munching mulberry leaves
on silk farms;
it nuzzles my plucked armpits like fat dogs;
it plays me
like a piano being played
by regimented fingers
through pressed sheets;
it walks across my back
like geese at dawn,
or the gentle manners
of my only nurse,
who handles me like glass, or Bethlehem.

My skin is white.
I neither eat nor sleep.
My only desire's a desire
to be free from desire.

Cow

I want to be a cow
and not my mother's daughter.
I want to be a cow
and not in love with you.
I want to feel free to feel calm.
I want to be a cow who never knows
the kind of love you 'fall in love with' with;
a queenly cow, with hips as big and sound
as a department store,
a cow the farmer milks on bended knee,
who when she dies will feel dawn
bending over her like lawn to wet her lips.

I want to be a cow,
nothing fancy –
a cargo of grass,
a hammock of soupy milk
whose floating and rocking and dribbling's undisturbed
by the echo of hooves to the city;
of crunching boots;
of suspicious-looking trailers parked on verges;
of unscrupulous restaurant-owners
who stumble, pink-eyed, from stale beds
into a world of lobsters and warm telephones;
of streamlined Japanese freighters
ironing the night,
heavy with sweet desire like bowls of jam.

The Tibetans have 85 words for states of consciousness.
This dozy cow I want to be has none.
She doesn't speak.
She doesn't do housework or worry about her appearance.
She doesn't roam.
Safe in her fleet
of shorn-white-bowl-like friends,
she needs, and loves, and's loved by,
only this –
the farm I want to be a cow on too.

Don't come looking for me.
Don't come walking out into the bright sunlight
looking for me,
black in your gloves and stockings and sleeves
and large hat.
Don't call the tractorman.
Don't call the neighbours.
Don't make a special fruit-cake for when I come home:
I'm not coming home.
I'm going to be a cowman's counted cow.
I'm going to be a cow
and you won't know me.

What Do I Really Believe?

I believe that Benedictine
tastes like a meteor;

I believe that antitheses and hyperboles
dilate like slowly eaten fruit;

I believe that when a man takes long, deep breaths
he is trying not to prematurely ejaculate;

that tangerines are oranges, and full of juice,
and do not move unless they are being carried;

that the idea of repelling the rabbits
with moth flakes was not a success;

that abbatoirs binge
on Santa Gertrudis bulls;

that if I meet someone I like,
I start to do it unconsciously;

that a prisoner is painting the bars of his cell sky-blue,
and a tall giraffe is living in a summer-house in Maine;

that Beethoven was so deaf
he thought he was a painter;

that giant slugs
can be bigger than chihuahuas;

that I always seem to get
the wrong end of the stick;

that I love you very much,
but it doesn't seem to make the slightest difference;

that it's all very well
but why don't you love me too?

that there ought to be a law against chihuahuas,
that no one has to groom a giant slug.

FRANCES HOROVITZ

Child in Cornwall
(for Adam Horovitz)

in his thrush-warm skull seabirds bleed white over the streets
their feathers drifting like knives
swan-boat and dragon in a whirlpool of stone

in an old house upon old stones he stands
colliding the sky with the bird
cows jump out of the oracular fields
the purple flower is the heart flower
its juice is distilled in his mouth
he sings with the sound of the fox

in his night-bed he floats up the long hill
over his eyes in water, his spilled cup spreading tides
his body the one white wave riding the ship
into the dragon harbour and out again
under the black castle on the stone cliff

in his hands the dead walk timeless in the wind-ridden grass
he has scattered their door-stones with flowers
and pried out the mouse bones from the ancient hearth

his veins are consumed with light
they flare out to the sun
as he runs over the straight roads to the space of the sea

through his mother's green ring he calls home the tide

he has answered the stones

he whimmers in sleep
for the blood-rocking of the endless boat
and a white bird crying over the white sea

Rain – Birdoswald

I stand under a leafless tree
more still, in this mouse-pattering
    thrum of rain,
than cattle shifting in the field.
    It is more dark than light.
A Chinese painter's brush of deepening grey
    moves in a subtle tide.

The beasts are darker islands now.
Wet-stained and silvered by the rain
    they suffer night,
marooned as still as stone or tree.
    We sense each other's quiet.

Almost, death could come
inevitable, unstrange
    as is this dusk and rain,
and I should be no more
    myself, than raindrops
glimmering in last light
    on black ash buds

or night beasts in a winter field.

Brigomaglos, a Christian, Speaks...

'Some say they saw the Bull,
stamping under the skyline
with the new sun rising between his horns.
They say the black blood flows like water...

I don't believe them.
It was only the officers,
    never the men
(any god would do for us
    till the White Christ came).
They'd see anything, anyway,
stumbling out of their caves
dizzy with darkness and the stink of blood.

Strange how they thought they brought the light to birth.

We pulled their temple down in the end,
opened it up to the proper light
– plenty of black birds flapping around
but never their Raven that flies to the sun.

We have the Sun,
our Christ is the Son who is brought to birth.
He is a white Dove
who walks in fields of light,
brighter than snow-light or water-light.
His light burns in us.
He has engraved our souls like glass
to hold his seeds of light.

Those old gods should keep their place
under the dark of stones
or in the deep wood.
They should fade like the last wood-ember
or the last sputtering flame of the lamp,
be echoed only in children's songs.

In sleep they crowd
riding the uneasy edge of dreams...'

The Mithraic Temple at Carrawburgh is believed
to have been pulled down by Christians in A.D. 297.

January

A sealed stillness
– only the stream moves,
tremor and furl of water
under dead leaves.

In silence
the wood declares itself:
angles and arabesques of darkness,
branch, bramble,
tussocks of ghost grass
– under my heel
ice shivers
frail blue as sky
between the runes of trees.

Far up
rooks, crows
flail home.

Evening

Lilac blossom crests the window sill
mingling whiteness with the good dark of this room.
A bloom of light hangs delicately in white painted angles.
Bluebells heaped in a pot
still hold their blue against the dark;
I see their green stalks glisten.

Thin as a swan's bone
I wait for the lessons of pain and light.
Grief is a burden, useless.
It must dissolve into the dark.
I see the hills, luminous.
There will be the holly tree
the hawthorn with mistletoe
foxgloves springing in thousands.

The hills also will pass away
                will remain
as this lilac light, these blue bells,
the good dark of this room.

KATHLEEN JAMIE

The way we live

Pass the tambourine, let me bash out praises
to the Lord God of movement, to Absolute
non-friction, flight, and the scarey side:
death by avalanche, birth by failed contraception.
Of chicken tandoori and reggae, loud, from tenements,
commitment, driving fast and unswerving
friendship. Of tee-shirts on pulleys, giros and Bombay,
barmen, dreaming waitresses with many fake-gold
bangles. Of airports, impulse, and waking to uncertainty,
to strip-lights, motorways, or that pantheon –
the mountains. To overdrafts and grafting

and the fit slow pulse of wipers as you're
creeping over Rannoch, while the God of moorland
walks abroad with his entourage of freezing fog,
his bodyguard of snow.
Of endless gloaming in the North, of Asiatic swelter,
to launderettes, anecdotes, passions and exhaustion,
Final Demands and dead men, the skeletal grip
of government. To misery and elation; mixed,
the sod and caprice of landlords.
To the way it fits, the way it is, the way it seems
to be: let me bash out praises – pass the tambourine.

Fountain

What are we doing when we toss a coin,
just a 5p-piece into the shallow dish
of the fountain in the city-centre
shopping arcade? We look down
the handrail of the escalator
through two-three inches of water
at a scatter of coins: round, flat, worthless,
reflections of perspex foliage
and a neon sign – *Fountain*.

So we glide from mezzanine to ground,
laden with prams, and bags printed
Athena, Argos, Olympus; thinking: now
in Arcadia est I'll besport myself
at the water's edge with kids,
coffee in a polystyrene cup.
We know it's all false: no artesian well
really leaps through strata
fathoms under *Man at C&A*, but
which of us can thrust her wrists
into a giggling hillside spring
above some ancient city?
So we flick in coins, show the children how:
make a wish! What for, in the shopping mall?
A wee stroke of luck? A something else, a nod
toward a goddess we almost sense
in the verdant plastic? Who says
we don't respond; can't still feel,
as it were, the dowser's twitch
up through the twin handles of the buggy.

The Queen of Sheba

Scotland, you have invoked her name
just once too often
in your Presbyterian living rooms.
She's heard, yea
even unto heathenish Arabia
your vixen's bark of poverty, come down
the family like a lang neb, a thrawn streak,
a wally dug you never liked
but can't get shot of.

She's had enough. She's come.
Whit, tae this dump? Yes!
She rides first camel
of a swaying caravan
from her desert sands
to the peat and bracken
of the Pentland hills

across the fit-ba pitch
to the thin mirage
of the swings and chute; scattered with glass.

Breathe that steamy musk
on the Curriehill Road, not mutton-shanks
boiled for broth, nor the chlorine stink
of the swimming pool where skinny girls
accuse each other of verrucas.
In her bathhouses women bear
warm pot-bellied terracotta pitchers
on their laughing hips.
All that she desires, whatever she asks –
she will make the bottled dreams
of your wee lasses
look like *sweeties*.

Spangles scarcely cover
her gorgeous breasts, hanging gardens
jewels, frankincense; more voluptuous
even than Vi-next-door, whose
high-heeled slippers
keeked from dressing gowns
like little hooves, wee tails
of pink fur stuffed in the cleavage of her toes;
more audacious even than Currie Liz
who led the gala floats
through the Wimpey scheme
in a ruby-red Lotus Elan
before the Boys' Brigade band
and the Brownies' borrowed coal-truck;
hair piled like candy-floss;
who lifted her hands from the neat wheel
to tinkle her fingers
at her tricks
          among the Masons and the elders and the police.

The cool black skin
of the Bible couldn't hold her,
nor the atlas green
on the kitchen table,
you stuck with thumbs
and split to fruity hemispheres

yellow Yemen, Red Sea, *Ethiopia*. Stick in
with the homework and you'll be
cliver like yer faither
but no too cliver,
no *above yersel*.

See her lead those great soft camels
widdershins round the kirk-yaird,
smiling
as she eats
avocados with apostle spoons
she'll teach us how. But first

she wants to strip the willow
she desires the keys
            to the National Library
she is beckoning
      the lasses
      in the awestruck crowd...

Yes, we'd like to
            clap the camels,
to smell the spice,
to admire her hairy legs and
bonny wicked smile, we want to take
PhDs in Persian, be vice
to her president: we want
to help her ask some
            Difficult Questions

she's shouting for our wisest man
to test her mettle:

      Scour Scotland for a Solomon!

Sure enough: from the back of the crowd
someone growls:
                  whae do you think y'ur?

and a thousand laughing girls
draw our hot breath
            and shout:

THE QUEEN OF SHEBA!

ELIZABETH JENNINGS

Transformation

Always I trip myself up when I try
To plan exactly what I'll say to you.
I should allow for how my feelings lie
Ready to leap up, showing what is true,

But in a way I never had designed.
How is it you are always ready when
Those linked ideas like beads within my mind
Break from their thread and scatter tears again?

I am amazed, and distances depart,
Words touch me back to quiet. I am free
Who could not guess such misery would start

And stop so quickly, change the afternoon
And, far much more than that, transfigure me.
Trusting myself, I enter night, stars, moon.

Rembrandt's Late Self-Portraits

You are confronted with yourself. Each year
The pouches fill, the skin is uglier.
You give it all unflinchingly. You stare
Into yourself, beyond. Your brush's care
Runs with self-knowledge. Here

Is a humility at one with craft.
There is no arrogance. Pride is apart
From this self-scrutiny. You make light drift
The way you want. Your face is bruised and hurt
But there is still love left.

Love of the art and others. To the last
Experiment went on. You stared beyond
Your age, the times. You also plucked the past
And tempered it. Self-portraits understand,
And old age can divest,

With truthful changes, us of fear of death.
Look, a new anguish. There, the bloated nose,
The sadness and the joy. To paint's to breathe,
And all the darknesses are dared. You chose
What each must reckon with.

Not for Use

A little of Summer spilled over, ran
In splashes of gold on geometry slates.
The grass unstiffened to pressure of sun.
I looked at the melting gates

Where icicles dropped a twinkling rain,
Clusters of shining in early December,
Each window a flaring, effulgent stain.
And easy now to remember

The world's for delight and each of us
Is a joy whether in or out of love.
'No one must ever be used for use,'
Was what I was thinking of.

Into the Hour

I have come into the hour of a white healing.
Grief's surgery is over and I wear
The scar of my remorse and of my feeling.

I have come into a sudden sunlit hour
When ghosts are scared to corners. I have come
Into the time when grief begins to flower

Into a new love. It had filled my room
Long before I recognised it. Now
I speak its name. Grief finds its good way home.

The apple-blossom's handsome on the bough
And Paradise spreads round. I touch its grass.
I want to celebrate but don't know how.

I need not speak though everyone I pass
Stares at me kindly. I would put my hand
Into their hands. Now I have lost my loss

In some way I may later understand.
I hear the singing of the summer grass.
And love, I find, has no considered end,

Nor is it subject to the wilderness
Which follows death. I am not traitor to
A person or a memory. I trace

Behind that love another which is running
Around, ahead. I need not ask its meaning.

The Way of Words and Language

When you are lost
Even near home, when you feel
The tide turning, a strange sea under you
And you are a pale, rubbed pebble, a sea ghost,

When you have lost
All the highways and every dimming sign-post
And the sea is far away and the moon hidden
And your watch has stopped and you have no compass
And feel to yourself like a ghost,

All this later will seem your best
Time for there will be future and memory and the tossed
Tide. Morning will come up and you will open your eyes
And see in the mirror a ghost.

But day will take you and the dawn uncover
The ribbed sand foot by foot and the first light
Will stretch over the grey water and you will know
It is no longer night

But still a time of silence and light like a shielded lamp.
Then you will shake off dreams and recover
What you know is yourself still but changed
And the new sun will come up and pass over
Your hands, your arms, your face and you will discover
A world that the night has re-arranged.

Let this time be. Let the present stay. Do not
Look back. Do not look forward. Let thought
Idle from dream into daylight, and watch, then, the coast
Climb out to dark, to grey, and then to chalk-white
Cliffs till the grey sea goes blue
And then indeed you

Are found and safe at last
And all your thought will grow
And you will unreel it, a silk thread, a long-
Travelling, moving-everywhere line
And it will gradually, as you relax. it, become a song
And you will not say 'That is mine'.

JENNY JOSEPH

Women at Streatham Hill

They stand like monuments or trees, not women,
Heavy and loaded on the common's edge
Pausing before the leaves' decline; far off
The railway runs through grass and bushes where
Slim girls and interested lovers seem
Another species, not just generation:
Butterflies flitting in the leaves, not stones.

> Nobody asks what they have done all day
> For who asks trees or stones what they have done?
> They root, they gather moss, they spread, they are.
> The busyness is in the birds about them.
> It would seem more removal than volition
> If once they were not there when men came home.

Ah giggling creamy beauties, can you think
You will withdraw into this private world
Weighted with shopping, spreading hands and feet,
Trunk gnarling, weatherworn? that if you get
All that your being hurls towards, like Daphne
Your sap will rise to nourish other things
Than suppliant arms and hair that glints and beckons?
Your bodies are keyed and spry, yet do you see
*Any*thing clearly through the grass-green haze
Hear anything but the murmur of desires?

> Bargains in bags, they separate towards home,
> Their talk a breeze that rustles topmost leaves
> Tickles the dust in crannies in the rock:
> Beetles that grind at roots it touches not.
> The women pull their thoughts in, easing like stones
> Where they are set, hiding the cavities.
> They care as little now to be disturbed
> As flighty daughters urgently want peace.

Language teaching: naming

Why are we frightened of the word for love?
We feast our eyes on eyes that light the soul.
The word is not more perilous than the dreams
We live on, poisoning the system.
We are not frightened of the acts of love.

I walked along an unfamiliar road
And all around, the birds twittered and danced
Through hedgerows blowing in a flatland wind.
I wished I knew their names and then instead
Of saying 'small, brown, with a spearing beak,
Taking a little run then going back,
Twittering a note that rose to a whistle then sank,
You know, those birds you see in hedgerows
Somewhere along the roads from Hertfordshire'
I could say 'thirp' or whatever bird it was,
And you would know in an instant what they were
How looked, what doing. I'd have caught the birds
In that one word, its name, and all the knowledge
You might have had that I'm not master of
Would straight away be there to help me out.
Naming is power, but now
The birds twitter and dance, change and so escape me.

Why are we frightened of the sound called love?
We talk quite freely about what we need,
We risk enormous punishment when we must.
Is this the word made flesh, rising to grasp us?
You'd think the act made flesh would impinge more
Than a tiny breath made actual through the voice box.
Grammar is power, is witchcraft, is enchantment.
Droplets and air rise from our lungs like a genie
Twisting huge from a bottle to fill a room.
Say 'love' not 'like' (changing tight voiceless sounds
Only a little to get that deep voiced 'v')
The iron gate clangs behind you, and beyond
The bridge in flames, swamps and no road ahead.
We only stay alive on what the word means
So why are we frightened of the name of love?

Dawn walkers

Anxious eyes loom down the damp–black streets
Pale staring girls who are walking away hard
From beds where love went wrong or died or turned away,
Treading their misery beneath another day
Stamping to work into another morning.

In all our youths there must have been some time
When the cold dark has stiffened up the wind
But suddenly, like a sail stiffening with wind,
Carried the vessel on, stretching the ropes, glad of it.

But listen to this now: this I saw one morning.
I saw a young man running, for a bus I thought,
Needing to catch it on this murky morning
Dodging the people crowding to work or shopping early.
And all heads stopped and turned to see how he ran
To see would he make it, the beautiful strong young man.
Then I noticed a girl running after, calling out 'John'.
He must have left his sandwiches I thought.
But she screamed 'John wait'. He heard her and ran faster,
Using his muscled legs and studded boots.
We knew she'd never reach him. 'Listen to me John.
Only once more' she cried. 'For the last time, John, please wait,
          please listen.'
He gained the corner in a spurt and she
Sobbing and hopping with her red hair loose
(Made way for by the respectful audience)
Followed on after, but not to catch him now.
Only that there was nothing left to do.

The street closed in and went on with its day.
A worn old man standing in the heat from the baker's
Said 'Surely to God the bastard could have waited.'

Living off other people – Welfare

It would be pretty to have roses
Flourishing by my back door.
It would be nice to have a well-kept house
With velvet chairs not scraping a polished floor.
It would be lovely to sit down at dinner
Grey tie, pearl pin, fresh shirt and well-kept hands
And good to have a purring car in a clean garage
Eye-catching as the best brass bands.

But to keep it all going would be a lot of worry
And anyone who does it has to race and scurry
Seeing to roofs and pruning, maintenance and mechanics,
A shower of rain, a little green fly, bring on terrible panics
And ruin and failure shadow every path.

So I think this is the best thing to do:
As I walk down roads I see so many flowers
Nod-nodding in all the gardens that I pass.
I can glance into other people's rooms that they have furnished
And look how courteously that man is turning
To open the front door to his gleaming house.
Did you see how his suit fitted him, his perfect cuffs? Spotless cars
Slide by with women in furs and perfumes
Wafted to me with the flavour of cigars.

I am wrapped in my layers of shapeless coats
And I need never polish or dig or set
The table out for four distinguished guests
Or get to an office or prove myself each day
To provide for hammocks and lawns,
To get my antiques protected against insects.
A guest everywhere, I look in as dinner is served.
As I tramp past others' gardens, the rose opens.

If you can't join them beat them
FROM *Life and Turgid Times of A. Citizen*

I have finished with saying I'm sorry and waiting
While badly-driven sports cars cross my path
Their thin-lipped drivers glaring and shouting 'Fuck you!'
Nor do I lower my window now only to be harangued
By some yellow-eyed little runt who only knows
'You oughtn't to be on the road, you ought to be shot.'

I content myself by thinking how they'll wear their pants out
Stuck to their seats encased in their only armour,
Fish that must flop on land, legs useless as penguins',
And that the pulse in their ticking cheeks probably means
Apoplexy at forty.
I used to boil in silence under the shock.
Now I open up the throttle and yell back.

SYLVIA KANTARIS

To a poet's anxious girlfriend

*I am going steady with an engineer who
wants to marry me. I thought he was ideal
until I found out that he writes poetry in his
spare time. Do you think I can depend on him?*
BRISBANE NEWSPAPER AGONY COLUMN

No wonder you're concerned.
Who wouldn't be?
Now it's in its early stages but,
like drink,
drugs
and other, furtive vices,
it's liable to get a hold on him
and end up colouring his life.

It tends to start as mere
belated adolescent bravado or
compensation for a nervous twitch or stammer.
At first it's only once a week, but soon it's
every day and finally
nights too.
He'll burn holes in the plastic walls of your tidy dreams
and let the wind in
if you don't watch him.

Besides which he's liable to
give up mothballs,
eat the telly,
grow his hair and fingers and
install kaleidoscopes on hire purchase.
What begins as a spare-time hobby
will eventually affect his senses,
and yours (it's contagious).

So all in all I'd advise you to
stay clear of the man
unless you can
get him to have treatment before it goes any further.
In its later stages it's terrible and
quite incurable.

Annunciation

It seems I must have been more fertile than most
to have taken that wind-blown
thistledown softly-spoken word
into my body and grown big-bellied with it.
Nor was I the first: there had been
rumours of such goings-on before my turn
came – tales of swansdown. Mine
had no wings or feathers actually
but it was hopeless trying to convince them.
They like to think it was a mystical
encounter, although they must know
I am not of that fibre – and to say I was
'troubled' is laughable.
What I do remember is a great rejoicing,
my body's arch and flow, the awe,
and the ringing and singing in my ears –
and then the world stopped for a little while.
But still they will keep on about the Word,
which is their name for it, even though I've
told them that is definitely
not how I would put it.
I should have known they'd try to take
possession of my ecstasy and
swaddle it in their portentous terminology.
I should have kept it hidden in the dark
web of my veins...
Though this child grows in me –
not unwanted certainly, but
not intended on my part; the risk
did not concern me at the time, naturally.
I must be simple to have told them anything.
Just because I stressed the miracle of it
they've rumoured it about the place that I'm
immaculate – but then they always were afraid
of female sexuality.
I've pondered these things lately in my mind.
If they should canonise me
(setting me up as chaste and meek and mild)
God only knows what nonsense
they'll visit on the child.

Still

I watch you mouthing angry words like somebody
in water behind glass, noting how your faults,
most of all, are magnified in close up.
Your skin ripples loose along your cheek-bones
as if you were about to shrug it off.
On my side, I no longer try to emulate
that underwater swimmer in the fifties film,
smiling, open-mouthed, as she approached
her technicolor lover and embraced him,
entangling arms and legs with his
and neither of them struggling to escape.
They seemed perfectly at home in a fish-tank
as in a fairy-tale, the water striped
with sunlight and her hair spun out like silk.
Even in the stills tonight, although they are
no longer larger-than-life, having shrunk to fit
the TV screen, and even though they both died
in between, their smiles are still as smooth as celluloid.
Watching them together, I could almost believe
that in order to stay happy-ever-after
we also should have learnt how not to breathe.

Toy Boy

*Men now outnumber women in the 16-35 age group
by 212,000. The toy boy phenomenon could make sense.*
THE OBSERVER

Why don't you try one? Mine's a lot of fun.
I turn the key and wind him up. He whirrs.
His clockwork heart ticks very, very fast,
as fast as mine, almost. Alas, the mechanism
of my own's so rusty, I expect the strain
of this new spring is bound to crack it up.

(An out-of-date model, madam; breakages
should be expected when antiques are fitted
with new parts. You're lucky yours has stood the pace
so long. It's not worth anything of course,
unless its sentimental value to yourself.)

Meanwhile my toy boy plucks the rubber bands
that keep my head hooked to my neck and the rest.
(I disassembled all my dolls; the worst
kept saying 'Mama' till I cut the crap
with scissors. All of them were sexless
except celluloid Kewpies which announced the Barbie Age.)

Last night I tried to take my new toy boy to bits,
thinking he might be an Action Man in camouflage,
but he said he couldn't cope with a Kalashnikov.
'O brave new world!' I tried to say, but gagged
when he told me he'd have to cut my head off
if I couldn't keep my trap shut and stop winding him up.

JACKIE KAY

Close Shave

The only time I forget is down the pit
right down in the belly of it,
my lamp shining like a third eye,
my breath short and fast like my wife's
when she's knitting. Snip snap.
I've tried to tell her as many times
as I've been down this mine. I can't
bring myself to, she'd tell our girls
most probably. It doesn't bear thinking.

Last night he shaved me again.
Close. Such an act of trust.
And he cut my hair; the scissors snip
snipped all night as I lay beside Ella
(Good job she's not that interested)
I like watching him sweep it up.
He holds the brush like a dancing partner,
short steps, fox trot: 4/4 time.
I knew from the first time, he did too

Our eyes met when he came
to the bit above my lip. 6 years ago.
We've only slept the night together twice:
once when my wife's sister died,
once when the brother-in-law committed suicide.
She left our daughters behind that time.
My nerves made me come too quick
but I liked sleeping in his smooth arms
till dawn. He was gone

Before they woke, giggling round breakfast.
He says nobody else can cut my curls.
I laughed loud for the first time since
God knows when. You're too vain man.
We kissed, I like his beard on my skin,
how can you be a barber with a beard
I said to him; it's my daughters that worry me.
Course I can never tell the boys down the pit.
When I'm down here I work fast so it hurts.

The Red Graveyard

There are some stones that open in the night like flowers.
Down in the red graveyard where Bessie haunts her lovers.
There are stones that shake and weep in the heart of night
Down in the red graveyard where Bessie haunts her lovers.

Why do I remember the blues?
I am five or six or seven in the back garden;
the window is wide open;
her voice is slow motion through the heavy summer air.
Jelly roll. Kitchen man. Sausage roll. Frying pan.

Inside the house where I used to be myself,
her voice claims the rooms. In the best room even,
something has changed the shape of my silence.
Why do I remember her voice and not my own mother's?
Why do I remember the blues?

My mother's voice. What was it like?
A flat stone for skitting. An old rock.
Long long grass. Asphalt. Wind. Hail.
Cotton. Linen. Salt. Treacle.
I think it was a peach.
I heard it down to the ribbed stone.

I am coming down the stairs in my father's house.
I am five or six or seven. There is fat thick wallpaper
I always caress, bumping flower into flower.
She is singing. (Did they play anyone else ever?)
My father's feet tap a shiny beat on the floor.

Christ, my father says, that's some voice she's got.
I pick up the record cover . And now. This is slow motion.
My hand swoops, glides, swoops again.
I pick up the cover and my fingers are all over her face.
Her black face. Her magnificent black face.
That's some voice. His shoes dancing on the floor.

There are some stones that open in the night like flowers
Down in the red graveyard where Bessie haunts her lovers.
There are stones that shake and weep in the heart of night
Down in the red graveyard where Bessie haunts her lovers.

Other Lovers

1 *What was it you said again there by the river*

And later, when the young danced to an old song,
the moon split in two, the stars smashed,
what was it again?

By the river, by the procession of trees,
the shadow marching across your face,
how deep do you feel?

I hold the light between us. Kiss you
hard in the dark. Ahead of us, the bright blue eyes of sheep.
Are there words for this? Words that sink to the bottom

of the river where ducks flap their sudden wings,
startle silence; believe me, believe me.
We walk this night, shining our bright eye ahead.
Do you love me, love me, do you.

2 *The Day You Change*

The lace curtains go up.
She starts saying *you always say;*
you realise you always do.
On the living wall, strange shapes spread
like those on hospital sheets.

She closes the curtain round herself;
you hold your hand against the side of your cheek.
Tonight, you eat an instant meal
(no long spaghetti, no candles.)
Conversation limited

to *pass the pepper.* In the bedroom
the cover is stretched taut,
pulled back and forth in a battle,
till the small hours leaves one of you cold.
How long is a night like this?

3 *When you move out*

You mark each box with a thick black pen.
You will always be neat, no matter what's said.
And fair. You do not pack what is not yours.
Even the joint presents: the Chinese vase,
the white dinner plates, the samovar,
you leave to her. You won't miss things.

At night you will lie on a different side.
Listen to another station to send you to sleep.
You will never play Nina Simone, again.
Other things won't be possible. Restaurants,
parks, cinemas, pubs. Avoid them. They are dangerous.
Never go near another garden. There's no point,

growing peonies to blossom without you. Delphiniums.
Take up something else. *It doesn't matter what.*

4 *Swim*

So, at the end of a perfect rainbow
you have upped and left, and I
have taken to swimming a hundred
lengths of breast-stroke per day.
This is the way of love.
Even swimming, I am obsessed
with the way your feet arc
when stroked, your legs,
the long length of them,
how I could have you all worked
up in seconds. My fingers
doing the butterfly, you saying,
Don't stop Don't stop Don't stop.

5 *She never thought she could with anyone else*

And now, here she is, whispering urgently into another ear.
Holding someone else tight. After the sixth month,
she returns the *I love you*, she's heard since day one.
In your island she lies in the sun like a traitor.
But you are always standing on her shoulders.
She starts to do things the way you did them.
She stacks dishes in order of size.

She begins to like your favourite cheese.
In restaurants she chooses the wine you chose.
She finds herself getting irritated
at the way her new lover makes a bed.
She misses smooth corners, no creases.
She scrubs the bath twice a day, and at night,
sees the wrong lover mouthing her name.

6 *Worse than that*

One day you find you are your other lover.
You use exactly the same expressions,
like a child uses its mothers.
You disapprove of the same things. Refuse
to laugh at certain jokes. Uncertain
of yourself now, you start to imitate an absence.
You don't know what to think of the News.
Your world lacks gravity. Her presence.
You drop yourself from a height. Don't fall.
You are scared to go from A to B
– she was the map-reader.
You're scared of new things to eat.
You poke at them on your plate, depressed.
Long for your favourite meal, a simple life;

until you learn to cook on your own
and it's good (though you say it yourself).
Out and about, you are so confident
you're taking short cuts, back alleys,
winding your way past yourself,
up a narrow cobbled close into the big High Street.
You stand, looking down, the air bursting
through your raincoat like a big balloon.
You manage to fathom one of those machines. *Easy.*
Catch your slick tenners, *No bother,*
and saunter off, whistling to yourself.

You have actually done it.
You would never have believed it.
You have a whole new life.

MIMI KHALVATI

Amanuensis

Mirza, scribe me a circle beneath
the grid that drew Columbus
from isle to isle, tipped the scale,
measured a plus and minus

in our round lives. Amanuensis,
do you hear me? Look at the tree
holding the sky in its arms, the earth
in its bowels. Oh, draw me

the rings in its bark, a beaded spiral
where I may walk on Persian
carpets woven in hues from sandbanks
where goats graze and the melon

cools in the stream. Have you seen the dome
of the mosque? Our signatures are there,
among galaxies, infinities: an incredulity
that leads even infidels to prayer!

The pool in the square is green with twine.
The tiles in the arch are floods
of blue brocade. And those painted stars
in the vault, this hive of hoods

and white arcades, are the stars and the sky
I saw on a night in Spain:
coves of milk and stalactites; the very same.
So leave your sacks of grain

my Mirza, your ledgers and your abacus. Turn back
to brighter skills than these:
your mirrors and mosaics. From each trapezium,
polygon, each small isosceles

face, extract me, entwine me. Be my double
helix! My polestar! My asterisks!
Nestle in my silences. But spell me out
and rhyme me in your lunes and arabesques!

The Waiting House

> *Tem Eyos Ki went to the waiting house to pass her sacred time in a*
> *sacred place, sitting on moss and giving her inner blood to the Earth*
> *Mother...she smiled, and sang...of a place so wondrous the minds*
> *of people could not even begin to imagine it...But sometimes a woman*
> *will think she hears a song, or thinks she remembers beautiful words,*
> *and she will weep a little for the beauty she almost knew. Sometimes*
> *she will dream of a place that is not like this one.*
>
> ANNE CAMERON
> Daughters of Copper Woman

And I will bring you sweetmeats of stars
                              and four leaf clover
and plait your hair in grassknot braid
                              that maidens weave
on holy days when streets are strewn
                              with widows' weeds;
and I will rub your spine with persian essence
                              rose and thyme
and stroke the down that tingling purrs of home.

And you will sing me songs my mother
                              used to sing
of pomegranates' stubborn juice sluiced
                              off silver trays
and rounded limbs in old hammams; and tales
                              of Taghi
at the kitchen-gate, gaunt and thin, slung
                              like a tinker's mule
with children's billycans, the smell of onion
                              taunting him.

And you will numb my rootless moan in murmurings,
                              bird of my breastbone
quieten, its sobbing still, its flailing wings;
                              and we will sit
in the waiting house, latticed by the sea,
                              in purdah drawn
by our sheet of hair, your cheekbone's arc
                              half-lit;
and we will croon and whisper till the hardening
                              yellow dawn

strikes on the mud where crabs peer out to pan
                              like periscopes;
then laying down on curling moss our ghosting
                              shadows' twine
in sieve of nature's palm, you will give me
                              your dreams
and I will give you mine and dreaming still
                              your blood
will live, as mine in yours, in mine.

Rubaiyat
(for Telajune)

Beyond the view of crossroads ringed with breath
her bed appears, the old-rose covers death
has smoothed and stilled; her fingers lie inert,
her nail-file lies beside her in its sheath.

The morning's work over, her final chore
was 'breaking up the sugar' just before
siesta, sitting cross-legged on the carpet,
her slippers lying neatly by the door.

The image of her room behind the pane,
though lost as the winding road shifts its plane,
returns on every straight, like signatures
we trace on glass, forget and find again.

I have inherited her tools: her anvil,
her axe, her old scrolled mat, but not her skill;
and who would choose to chip at sugar-blocks
when sugar-cubes are boxed beside the till?

The scent of lilacs from the road reminds me
of my own garden: a neighbouring tree
grows near the fence. At night its clusters loom
like lantern-moons, pearly-white, unearthly.

I don't mind that the lilac's roots aren't mine.
Its boughs are, and its blooms. It curves its spine
towards my soil and litters it with dying
stars: deadheads I gather up like jasmine.

My grandmother would rise and take my arm,
then sifting through the petals in her palm
would place in mine the whitest of them all:
'Salaam, dokhtaré-mahé-man, salaam!'

'Salaam, my daughter-lovely-as-the-moon!'
Would that the world could see me, Telajune,
through your eyes! Or that I could see a world
that takes such care to tend what fades so soon.

LIZ LOCHHEAD

In the Dreamschool

1 *In the Dreamschool*

you are never the teacher.
The history lesson
goes on for ever.

Yammering the always
wrong answer to the hardest question
you stand up in nothing but
a washed-in vest.

In the dreamschool nothing can be covered up.
Fleeced, yellowing
you never learn.

Teacher is big-eyed behind
awesome bifocals
and his teeth are green.
An offered apple will only tempt the snake
curled under his chalkstripe jacket. Loch-
gelly, forked tongue, tawse.
Moonfaced mongols drag you towards
the terrible lavatories.

Sawdust soaks up sour mistakes.

2 *The Teachers*

they taught
that what you wrote in ink
carried more weight than what you wrote in pencil
and could not be rubbed out.
Punctuation was difficult. Wars
were bad but sometimes necessary
in the face of absolute evil as they knew only too well.

Miss Prentice wore her poppy the whole month of November.
Miss Mathieson hit the loud pedal
on the piano and made us sing
The Flowers of the Forest.
Miss Ferguson deplored the Chinese custom
of footbinding but extolled the ingenuity
of terracing the paddy fields.
Someone she'd once known had given her a kimono and a parasol.
Miss Prentice said the Empire had enlightened people
and been a two-way thing.
The Dutch grew bulbs and were our allies in
wooden shoes.

We grew bulbs on the window sills
beside the frogspawn that quickened into wriggling
commas or stayed full stop.
Some people in our class were stupid, full stop.
The leather tawse was coiled around the sweetie tin
in her desk beside the box of coloured blackboard chalk
Miss Ferguson never used.

Miss Prentice wore utility smocks.
Miss Mathieson had a moustache.
If your four-needled knitting got no
further than the heel you couldn't turn
then she'd keep you at your helio sewing
till its wobbling cross-stitch was specked with rusty blood.

Spelling hard words was easy when you knew how.

3 *The Prize*

for Perfect Attendance was an easy one to win.
Bible stories for girls. Martha and Mary on the coloured frontispiece.
Your Sunday name in the Superintendent's copperplate.

It meant being there, not 'paying attention'.
The Redemption Hymnbook proved
the devil did not possess every best tune.

Red ticks like flyaway
flocks of birds sprigged the best exercise books.
Gold stars were favours given seldom as boiled sweets
in crinkled cellophane. Xs were kisses
and kissing was wrong as all my sums.
Being first was top desk.
The doltish and dirty shared front row
with one sent down clever chatterbox in easy reach
of the teacher's ruler.
That September the squirrel
on the Shell country calendar wasn't on the wall
before Mattie won first death.
The weather chart said Today it is Cloudy
and my Top in General Knowledge
came of knowing the name for such a cloud
was Cumulus. We had to all turn over our jotters
and go over and over once again
till we knew by heart the Highway Code.

The Grim Sisters

And for special things
(weddings, school-
concerts) the grown up girls next door
would do my hair.

Luxembourg announced Amami night.

I sat at peace passing bobbipins
from a marshmallow pink cosmetic purse
embossed with jazzmen,
girls with pony tails and a November
topaz lucky birthstone.
They doused my cow's-lick, rollered
and skewered tightly.
I expected that to be lovely
would be worth the hurt.

They read my Stars,
tied chiffon scarves to doorhandles, tried
to teach me tight dancesteps
you'd no guarantee
any partner you might find would ever be able to
keep up with as far as I could see.

There were always things to burn
before the men came in.

For each disaster
you were meant to know the handy hint.
Soap at a pinch
but better nailvarnish (clear) for ladders.
For kisscurls, spit.
Those days womanhood was quite a sticky thing
and that was what these grim sisters came to mean.

'You'll know all about it soon enough.'
But when the clock struck they
stood still, stopped dead.
And they were left there
out in the cold with the wrong skirt-length
and bouffant hair,
dressed to kill,

who'd been
all the rage in fifty-eight,
a swish of Persianelle,
a slosh of perfume.
In those big black mantrap handbags
they snapped shut at any hint of *that*
were hedgehog hairbrushes,
cottonwool mice and barbed combs to tease.
Their heels spiked bubblegum, dead leaves.

Wasp waist and cone breast, I see them yet.
I hope, I hope
there's been a change of more than silhouette.

G

MARION LOMAX

Her husband speaks to her of Dragons

Haruko, I give up my mind to you
To swell whatever space you now inhabit:
It swirls with the dragons of your silk kimono
Dipped in violence the dark cannot articulate.
Our daughter wrestles with it in the night
We both keep echoes to soothe such spasms –
Sometimes she starts, listens, as if your voice
Is being rung across the fields, calling her to sleep.
In the morning she wakes dry-eyed: I weep.

Your grandfather's sword still hangs where it did.
I will shame both our families if I cannot heal
This sickness of wanting what is denied.
On the door your empty clothes-hanger strikes
Your absence – one, two (softly), three…four.
It is not the goldfinches' glass song
Or that high plaintive music of your own
As you smoothed hair under tall combs –
But the stubborn rejection of wire by wood.

I have laid away everything you wore:
Even the familiar has grown hard,
Oppressing me with trivialities made cruel.
Help me to kill my desire, to think of you
As one who found a better love elsewhere.
Let me find a clue that you had plans
To be more than a mother and my wife.
If I thought you safe I could forgive
Even the base charade of death.

I need to know that this was ordained;
That like the branches of the cherry, you reach up
And are not lost in earth to a stale faith.
This girl here has your eyes, but not your soul:
She comforts and torments me with your smile.
We meet through her – for her sake, it must cease.
We must not let her stumble from our bed
To her own low mattress, flanked by dragons –
Lips set under the weight of your clothes.

The Forked Tree

I killed two hares last night in the heart of the garden.
Long ears in moonlight, mimicking the shape of the tree.
I crept round the side of the house before they sensed me
And when they heard the gun clear its throat it was too late.
I hit the buck first, then the doe – stupidly standing
To stare at me. Her powerful hindquarters refusing
To kick and run, though I knew she could have bounded up
The lane in an instant, back to her young. I can cope
With hares: they are easy to cook. I feel no remorse.
Now I'll wait for the vixen who raids the chicken house.

I feed my chickens. Gather and sort the eggs. I wipe
The dirt and straw collage from the shells of those I sell.
I have the dogs too. My husband trained them, but I was
Surprised how quickly they obeyed me. I talked to them –
More easily than I talked to the children. Could share
The shadow with its dark gun lurking by our house wall
And the silent bullet lodged inside before we knew
That it was growing. His coming out of hospital,
Then the sniper's second strike when he was off his guard.
In the end I could only stand stupidly and stare –

Even with warning, could not believe such treachery.
The children were swinging from the tree in the garden
With no one to catch them. Darkness made the ground tremble
With hooves which left the grass trampled and the roses spoiled.
I guard this warren – small rooms and scattered outbuildings.
Not even chickens shall live in fear of predators.
My children shall feed better than before. Lonely nights
Are not without fear, but I cope with darkness now that
I have seen it bring young deer down from the wood to play.
Jumping in and out in the moonlight, through the forked tree.

Last Traces

Light stitches the trees
In tapestry. They
Gleam in bright cottons
Stretched taut on a frame.
A needle gathers
The valley up in
A pucker of green.

The embroidery grows
More lush each season:
The mill has to fight
Its way though branches.
Chimneys are bobbins
For fast-winding vines
From runaway looms.

These defiant ruins
Spin out the silence
Round gossiping birds
And a busy stream.
There are no machines;
No women's voices;
Few remnants remain.

But where clogs clattered
Towards their shuttles
In the needle light
The lane is woven
With exotic weeds
Which came with the cotton
And refused to leave.

Beyond Men

Through the shrunk boards
water strokes itself:
dives at the ends of staves.
Her eyes are out to sea:
she's gardening the waves,
weeding out boats before
they can put down roots.

Off the beach, women
bob like seals in their
round red caps – climb out,
and dance with strangers.

Under the pier, where
the sea has slipped back,
the wet sand is coldest.
It sucks her shoulders,
makes her shiver.
Arms, legs, breasts, slip
under: she struggles
out of the strong embrace.
Sleek, salt tongues of weed
lick neck and nipples –
waves return her hair,
a tangle of black lace.

Dancers on the pier
drift home to their beds,
refusing late drinks
or a possessive caress.
Tonight the sea's moans
make women yearn
for something beyond
the love of men.

MEDBH McGUCKIAN

To My Grandmother

I would revive you with a swallow's nest:
For as long a time as I could hold my breath
I would feel your pulse like tangled weeds
Separate into pearls. The heart should rule
The summer, ringing like a sickle over
The need to make life hard. I would
Sedate your eyes with rippleseed, those
Hollow points that close as if
Your eyelids had been severed to
Deny you sleep, imagine you a dawn.
I would push a chrysanthemum stone
Into your sleeve without your noticing
Its reaching far, its going, its returning.
When the end of summer comes, it is
A season by itself; when your tongue
Curls back like a sparrow's buried head,
I would fill your mouth with rice and mussels.

The Aphrodisiac

She gave it out as if it were
A marriage or a birth, some other
Interesting family event, that she
Had finished sleeping with him, that
Her lover was her friend. It was his heart
She wanted, the bright key to his study,
Not the menacings of love. So he is
Banished to his estates, to live
Like a man in a glasshouse; she has taken to
A little cap of fine white lace
In the mornings, feeds her baby
In a garden you could visit blindfold
For its scent alone:
                    But though a ray of grace
Has fallen, all her books seem as frumpish

As the last year's gambling game, when she
Would dress in pink taffeta, and drive
A blue phaeton, or in blue, and drive
A pink one, with her black hair supported
By a diamond comb, floating about
Without panniers. How his most
Caressing look, his husky whisper suffocates her,
This almost perfect power of knowing
More than a kept woman. The between-maid
Tells me this is not the only secret staircase.
Rumour has it she's taken to rouge again.

From the Dressing-Room

Left to itself, they say, every foetus
Would turn female, staving in, nature
Siding then with the enemy that
Delicately mixes up genders. This
Is an absence I have passionately sought,
Brightening nevertheless my poet's attic
With my steady hands, calling him my blue
Lizard till his moans might be heard
At the far end of the garden. For I like
His ways, he's light on his feet and does
Not break anything, puts his entire soul
Into bringing me a glass of water.

I can take anything now, even his being
Away, for it always seems to me his
Writing is for me, as I walk springless
From the dressing-room in a sisterly
Length of flesh-coloured silk. Oh there
Are moments when you think you can
Give notice in a jolly, wifely tone,
Tossing off a very last and sunsetty
Letter of farewell, with strict injunctions
To be careful to procure his own lodgings,
That my good little room is lockable,
But shivery, I recover at the mere
Sight of him propping up my pillow.

The Hard Summer

Then I was one long curve, from
The top of my head to my toes,
And an unseen arm kept me from
Falling over. My locked line
Was a kind of sweep, like the letter
S, diffusing as it pulled away
The light that came from below.
Your fingers found how breast
And arm change when they press
Together, how the bent leg
Hides even from the married
The H behind the knee. Though
Certain bones lie always
Next to the skin, an elbow
Forcing the back to crease
Might just be playing 'The Hard
Summer' for us, like a gift
That passes from father to daughter.
All that is month-named is
The T-shape of your face in the
Spring shadows, folds in your palm
That fall aside like breasts,
Creating the letter M.

A Different Same

Moonlight is the clearest eye:
Moonlight as you know enlarges everything.
It occupies a pool so naturally
It might have grown there.
Its stoniness makes stones look less than us.
Our hands begin to feel like hooves
Deep in this life and not in any other.
It can free the crossed arms from the body
Where time has fitted them without question,
And place them once random in a swimming

Position, so it seems you have opened
Without sound. There are figures standing
On steps, and figures reading. Not one
Walks past without being blurred
Like bronze snapshots. The church bell hangs
In the swirling porthole of the yew tree,
Pierced by a sea as abstract and tough
As the infant around the next corner.
Morning, mid-morning, afternoon and evening,
The rose that is like a pink satin theatre
Programme spreads to three gardens
With her roots in one. Her gaze, from the intersection
Of the terrace, gathers in the horizon,
A ceiling of translucent planes
With paintings of fruit in each. Awake at night
Uprooted me from some last minute shoulder.
I came out of the photograph
With that year underneath this dream;
It met with his mouth.

Turning the Moon into a Verb

A timeless winter
That wants to be now
Will go on taking shape in me.
Now everything can begin.

Everything can reach much
Further up; with this new
Listening, the longing at the window
For the missing season weakens.

When springtime had need of him,
He did not offer me the winter,
He took away each of the seasons
In its visual turn.

Dark does that to you also,
And the headlessness
Of a turning of light that mentions a green
A little darker than all other greens.

A secret year, a secret time,
Its flight is a written image
Of its cry, its capacity for sound
I call spring, the experience

When the sky becomes a womb,
And a vision of rivers slanting
Across the doubly opened page
Of the moon turns her into a verb.

An image I have consciously
Broken like a shoulder on your hearing,
The inconstancy within constancy
That is the price of a month.

PAULA MEEHAN

Buying Winkles

My mother would spare me sixpence and say,
'Hurry up now and don't be talking to strange
men on the way.' I'd dash from the ghosts
on the stairs where the bulb had blown
out into Gardiner Street, all relief.
A bonus if the moon was in the strip of sky
between the tall houses, or stars out,
but even in rain I was happy – the winkles
would be wet and glisten blue like little
night skies themselves. I'd hold the tanner tight
and jump every crack in the pavement,
I'd wave up to women at sills or those
lingering in doorways and weave a glad path through
men heading out for the night.

She'd be sitting outside the Rosebowl Bar
on an orange-crate, a pram loaded
with pails of winkles before her.
When the bar doors swung open they'd leak
the smell of men together with drink
and I'd see light in golden mirrors.
I envied each soul in the hot interior.

I'd ask her again to show me the right way
to do *it*. She'd take a pin from her shawl –
'Open the eyelid. So. Stick it in
till you feel a grip, then slither him out.
Gently, mind.' The sweetest extra winkle
that brought the sea to me.
'Tell yer Ma I picked them fresh this morning.'

I'd bear the newspaper twists
bulging fat with winkles
proudly home, like torches.

Two Buck Tim from Timbuctoo

I found it in the granary under rubble
where the back gable caved in,
a 78 miraculously whole in a nest of smashed records,
as if it had been hatched by a surreal hen,
a pullet with a taste for the exotic.

I took it in and swabbed it down,
put it on the turntable and filled the cottage
with its scratchy din. Ghosts of the long dead
flocked from their narrow grooves beneath foreign soils
to foxtrot round my kitchen in the dusk.

I'd say Leitrim in the forties was every bit as depressed
as Leitrim is today, the young were heading off
in droves, the same rain fell all winter long.
Eventually one old woman was left looking at her hands
while the Bell Boys of Broadway played 'Two Buck Tim from
          Timbuctoo',

and dreamt her daughters back about the place, the swing of a skirt,
a face caught in lamplight, with every revolution of the disc.
This winter I have grown unduly broody. As I go
about my daily work an otherworldly mantra turns
within my head: Two Buck Tim from Timbuctoo,

Two Buck Tim from Timbuctoo. It keeps me up at night.
I roam about the rooms. I hope to catch them at it.
I want to rend the veil, step out onto their plane,
spiral down a rain-washed road, let some ghostly partner
take the lead, become at last another migrant soul.

The Man who Lives in the Clouds

You said if we reached the top
we'd find the navel of the earth,
proof that matter was a mere prop,
a gift, our right from birth,

to keep us occupied through time,
that energy alone was real.
I was breathless from the climb.
I wanted a bed and a decent meal.

I was sick of the dirt, the reek of yak
butter seeping from my haversack,
the prospect of another night,
the endless talk of humanity's plight,

of philosophers' stones and holy grails.
I wanted nothing more than to stand
humbly on the lower slopes and gaze
at the peaks, and whether I was damned

or saved was much of a muchness to me.
You claimed the dead lived deep inside
the mountain, that they clamoured to be free.
I heard only the wind lash like a tide

race through the trees. I left
you then and made for home, deaf
to your threats, your curses. Now
I lead a quiet life in the village below.

I've a clutch of hens, a herb patch, a video
and a black cat. I do not think of you
up there with your yetis, your eagles, your thunderbolts,
and your dense cloud cover the sun can't break through.

You Open Your Hands to Me

They hold nothing
They are calloused
Earth under the fingernails
The heart line strong and sure
As any river crazy for the sea

These hands hold nothing
They are the hands of a worker
They are the hands of one who has no job

They have tucked a whole city up at night
And in the morning cast it adrift

These hands could pack everything they value
In a minute or less

From a burning building
They would save what is living
Not what is Art

They reach to me in the dark
Of a nightmare
They pull me clear
They place the particular stars I prefer
At my window
On cloudy nights
They make images of the moon
In case I am lonely

These hands hold nothing
They do not judge
They are drawn to the wounded
They have no history
They fire the first shot

They are the hands of a builder
They dismantle empires
They love most what is wild
They invite no pity

Were I dying I would choose
These hands to guide me
Out of the world

You open your hands to me
Your empty hands

ELMA MITCHELL

Thoughts After Ruskin

Women reminded him of lilies and roses.
Me they remind rather of blood and soap,
Armed with a warm rag, assaulting noses,
Ears, neck, mouth and all the secret places:

Armed with a sharp knife, cutting up liver,
Holding hearts to bleed under a running tap,
Gutting and stuffing, pickling and preserving,
Scalding, blanching, broiling, pulverising,
– All the terrible chemistry of their kitchens.

Their distant husbands lean across mahogany
And delicately manipulate the market,
While safe at home, the tender and the gentle
Are killing tiny mice, dead snap by the neck,
Asphyxiating flies, evicting spiders,
Scrubbing, scouring aloud, disturbing cupboards,
Committing things to dustbins, twisting, wringing,
Wrists red and knuckles white and fingers puckered,
Pulpy, tepid. Steering screaming cleaners
Around the snags of furniture, they straighten
And haul out sheets from under the incontinent
And heavy old, stoop to importunate young,
Tugging, folding, tucking, zipping, buttoning,
Spooning in food, encouraging excretion,
Mopping up vomit, stabbing cloth with needles,
Contorting wool around their knitting needles,
Creating snug and comfy on their needles.

Their huge hands! their everywhere eyes! their voices
Raised to convey across the hullabaloo,
Their massive thighs and breasts dispensing comfort,
Their bloody passages and hairy crannies,
Their wombs that pocket a man upside down!

And when all's over, off with overalls,
Quickly consulting clocks, they go upstairs,
Sit and sigh a little, brushing hair,
And somehow find, in mirrors, colours, odours,
Their essences of lilies and of roses.

Vulnerable

Everything is vulnerable at sunrise.
Houses are blurred at the edge by the creeping light.
They are not yet upright, not yet property.

Inside the houses
Bodies and beds are still to be disentangled,
Naked, bearded, sheeted, flowing, breathing,
With no cosmetic except the morning's colouring.

No body has had time to put on its uniform
To arm itself with the safe and usual phrases,
To start counting, considering, feeling hungry,
Being man or woman...

They lie scattered, invisible, soft, lovable,
Under the surreptitious hands of the sunrise,
The touching light.

They are not yet upright, not yet property.

The Death of Adam

I saw it coming,
The cold.
It must have been coming on a long time.
Ever since I'd known him.

Not surprising, really,
With him come up from the dust
And me from the bone.

Still, it was odd,
Watching it actually happen.
Everything sags; did you know?
I didn't know.

Teeth fall out, and then the face falls in.
Skin
Withers and wrinkles and shrivels like an apple
(Yes, like an apple)
And the top of the skull
(Where the hair and the brains keep complicated house together)
Becomes
Plain, smooth, simple,
Unoccupied by anything.

And he couldn't walk at all, nor talk at all
(We had to stop arguing about whose fault it was)
And the sun made his eyes hurt
And he had to leave the world that belonged to him
And the animals he'd given a name to
And the wife that was part of him,
To become a kind of collapse,
A remnant, something remembered,
Not all there any more.

He was always first at everything
And now
The first man ever to be dead.
Perhaps, as gardeners,
We should have learned from the leaves
What it means to be deciduous.

Will it always be just like this
For the rest of us?
Or must I look forward
To a separate, feminine, suitable
Method of disappearance?
Middle-aged, but still naked
To man-stare and God-stare
Covering myself up with my hands and my long grey hair,
Breasts falling like apples
And the small pool of darkness
Inside me
Gone dry?

Country Life

Within half-a-mile, to my knowledge,
Two solitary alcoholics,
A divorce in progress,
Homes crumbling under nettles.

Badgers, nocturnally ambling,
The fox caught red-muzzled,
The owls hanging up night in inverted commas,
Molework.   The moon's partners.

Swamp waiting in patience
To suck down plough, or be ripped open.
Trees prevented from falling
Only by trees.   The furze-defended common.

Barbed-wire entanglement of stars. The river's
Gradual grovelling infiltration
Like a farm dog edging into the living-room.
And men.   And women.

GRACE NICHOLS

Because She Has Come

Because she has come
with geometrical designs
upon her breasts

Because she has borne five children
and her belly is criss-crossed
with little tongues of fire

Because she has braided her hair
in the cornrow, twisting it upwards
to show her high inner status

Because she has tucked
a bright wrap
about her Nubian brownness

Because she has stained her toes
with the juice of the henna
to attract any number of arrant males

Because she has the good sense
to wear a scarab
to protect her heart

Because she has a pearl
in the middle
of her lower delta

Give her honour
Give her honour, you fools,
Give her honour.

Configurations

He gives her all the configurations
of Europe

She gives him a cloud burst of parrots.

He gives her straight blond hairs
and a white frenzy.

She gives him black wool. The darkness
of her twin fruits.

He gives her uranium, platinum, aluminium
and concorde.

She gives him her 'Bantu buttocks'.

He rants about the spice in her skin.

She croons his alabaster and scratches him.

He does a Columbus –
falling on the shores of her tangled nappy orchard.

She delivers up the whole Indies again
But this time her wide legs close in
        slowly
Making a golden stool of the empire
of his head.

Abra-Cadabra

My mother had more magic
in her thumb
than the length and breadth
of any magician

Weaving incredible stories
around the dark-green senna brew
just to make us slake
the ritual Sunday purgative

Knowing when to place a cochineal poultice
on a fevered forehead
Knowing how to measure a belly's symmetry
kneading the narah pains away

Once my baby sister stuffed
a split-pea up her nostril
my mother got a crochet needle
and gently tried to pry it out

We stood around her
like inquisitive gauldings

Suddenly, in surgeon's tone she ordered,
'Pass the black pepper,'
and patted a little
under the dozing nose

My baby sister sneezed.
The rest was history.

Blackout

Blackout is endemic to the land.
People have grown sixth sense
and sonic ways, like bats,
emerging out of the shadows
into the light of their own flesh.

But the car headlamps coming towards us
make it seem we're in some third world movie,
throwing up potholes and houses exaggeratedly,
the fresh white painted and grey ramshackle
blending into snug relief.

And inside, the children are still hovering,
hopeful moths around – The flickerless Box,
immune to the cloying stench of toilets
that can't be flushed. The children,
all waiting on electric-spell to come
and trigger a movie, the one featuring America,
played out endlessly in their heads.

While back outside, coconut vendors decapitate
the night, husky heads cutlassed off
in the medieval glow of bottle lamps.

And everywhere there are flittings
and things coming into being,
in a night where footfall is an act of faith –
A group of young girls huddled
in a questionable doorway;
The sudden dim horizontal of an alleyway;
And the occasional generator-lit big house,
obscenely bright –
hurting the soft iris of darkness
in this worn-out movie, slow reeling

Under the endless cinema of the skies.

JULIE O'CALLAGHAN

Yuppie Considering Life in Her Loft Apartment

Jeff is such a bastard.
Like I can't handle it.
All I did was throw the silver fork
he'd left stuck for a week
in the mud at the base
of my weeping willow tree
in the general direction of his chest
and while it was en route added,
'What am I, your maid, lunkhead?'
He, as usual, moved *before* the fork
crash landed on his bicep and said,
'No prob, no prob', and those were
his last words to me on his way
out of my orbit and into the
gravitational pull of some dumb broad.
Advice has been pouring in:
'One look and I told you –
he's a no-goodnik, but you said you
liked his shoes, so there's no point
talking to you is there?';
and, 'Cancel him offa yer floppy disk,
revise your memory bank
and write a new programme –
who needs the louse anyway?';
and, 'Join the club. Ya wanna
come with me for a facial? –
Elizabeth Arden have a special offer.'
The part that really gets to me
is that I forgot everything I learned
in that Psychology course I took last year:
'The Male Ego and How to Cope With It'.

Matinee

Grandma, whisper, everybody's turning around.
– Well is she being thrown out of the convent?
No, she's just going to be a governess for a while.
– What does she have on?
A brown dress, hat and she's carrying a suitcase.
– Where's she going, is she walking or what?
Yeah, she's walking to the house where she's got the job.
– Why didn't they pick her up in a carriage?
So she could sing a song on the way.
– Is this a true story?
I guess so.
– Well I bet they picked her up.
Now she's meeting the family.
– She marries the father, Ingrid told me.
He's very handsome and rich.
– I thought you said she was still a nun.

Winter
(after Sei Shonagon)

I. *Empress Sadako Considers Snow*

When I wore my hair
straight across my forehead,
I loved deep drifts
in my father's yard.
We would spend all day
making a snow mountain,
praying to Goddess Shirayama
not to let it melt.
Now I stir the red embers
in my brazier, watching flurries
through the icy lattice
and have ordered that no one
disturb the snow outside my rooms
by shuffling wooden clogs there
or heaping it into a silly mountain.
Snow is shapeliest when left alone.

II. *Silver*

I'm the only one who seems to care anymore
about the Winter Festival at Kamo.
The evening should be cold enough for snow,
with bonfires, dancers and musicians.
First I hear the sound of drums,
then my eyes follow the light
from the flaming pine torches.
I am always overjoyed at the costumes
of lustrous silk, frozen stiff with ice
and the palace roof outlined in white
seems thatched in silver.
Everyone says, 'You get too excited.'
How can I help it?
I will stay up remembering
until the dawn bell.

III. *Men and Precipitation*

My dislike of rain is profound.
Your hair goes stringy,
mud cakes your shoes and hem
and the whole world
becomes a drippy damp
annoyingly stupid place.
But if a man arrives during a storm,
dressed in the yellow-green
of a Chamberlain
or, best of all, in a proper Court robe
moistened by sleet,
I can't hide my admiration.
I forget all about the hateful showers,
organise dry clothes, a warm drink
and pay careful attention
to wringing out his costume.
Nothing pleases me more
than a secret meeting
with a man covered in raindrops.

The Sounds of Earth
(broadcast from Voyager-II to the universe)

Here is the most popular sound first:
we call it talking – it is also known fondly as
shooting off one's mouth, discussing,
chewing the fat, yammering, blabbing,
conversing, confiding, debating, speaking,
gossiping, hollering and yakking.
So here's a whole bunch of jaw creakers.
How come none of you guys out there
don't yap at us – we'd sure like to hear
what you have to say
on the subject of where the hell you are.

For our second selection,
we will now play a medley of music
which you may or may not care for
since as I know myself
music is a very personal thing.
Why not aim a little musical extravaganza earthward?
As I say – we're waiting.

Now for our something-for-everyone finale.
Here's a rush hour traffic jam,
brakes are screeching – horns are blasting.
This is the phone ringing with typewriters
and computer printers in the background.
I'm very partial to this next one:
a rocking chair creaking on a porch
with birds and crickets chirping.
To finish up, we've got a lawn mower,
knitting needles, a hammer, a saw,
a football stadium after a score,
a door shutting, a baby crying
and a kitchen sink filling with water
for a cosmic thigh-slapper.

We're equal opportunity down here
so if you're a blob or have three heads
or look like something the cat dragged in –
we won't bat an eyelid.

RUTH PADEL

Amniocentesis

Walled princess of the knot-garden
glinting with fat red fruit,
dependent from an amethyst-black shining plait,
you approach without modesty, native
from a vulnerable heartland,
spiralled round wayward seed,
hooks of peppergrain on white of softboiled egg.
I lived my physiology unthinkingly till now.

Your small lungs breathe inner liquid,
as the Greeks supposed we do.
You make your own antiquity in me.
Fireflies of premonition gather in my stem.
Thoughts of a burning spine,
starfall–silver gooseflesh in a winter labour ward,
a tambourine for ancient winds of pain...
I know your chemistry, at least.

That needle, a precision hummingbird,
sipped your round world. The doctor's
green apprentice interleaved your chromosomes
in glass. With an animal's determined privacy
you guard your ticking dark. Floating,
you prepare to wring my heart. One lightbulb
builds the bedroom round us.
How will you change our lives?

Daylilies glow on the path to the shed.
Will I be able to pause as you come,
if rocks are steep by the tough
furred flanks of the waterfall?
Imagination labours on into the night
to a last parapet, that neolithic fear
something will stay unlived.
A foreign drink rustles on the stove.

The Starling

They are talking of trepanning the Indian starling
because the starling thinks she is the Empress of Oslo
and besides, she is very lonely. The Kissagram boy,
off duty, brought her in from the westwoods
under the flyover, her tertiaries dipped in ink:
smaragdine plus a lavender-cum-royal blue.

She looked, then, a bedraggled poisonous orchid.
We bled her at the hip or wherever roughly
you might expect a hip in all that tininess.
She lies alone on puffed flannel and can't sleep.
I've slipped out, nights, against orders
to feed her cinnamon toast, read her *The Golden Bough*.

Her eye is cloudy, suspicious. She voids phlegm
and half-dreams of a childless woman
killed in a bar in backstreet Friedenstadt,
and that nobody, nobody mourned her
as the starling thinks *she* should be mourned.
Bedlam's Managing Director, the one man

who can save our starling, has evaded diagnosis.
He says it was a present from the King.
After the first incision, he kept his scalpel
under the raw lid of its Royal Society box
in a self-shaped baize hollow like the bed
of a chestnut in its shell. Or a sharp empty egg.

Trepanning, bloodletting: early seventeenth-century cures for insanity.

Angel

No one sees me. Fathoms up
a nest of rays, all protein,
grey velvet triangles

six metres wing to wing,
a coat on them like a Vymerana,
ripples at the edges, slow,

the way the skite-tooth grass
trembled in lunar winds back home.
So no one knows

and if they read the impress
where my egg sacs
crumbled into bed, work done,

there's nothing they could do.
I listen to the humming
and I wait. Suppose they clawed

one ring from my antenna-bone
up through that tunnel of sea-cow
and acetta-swabs

changing sex halfway through life,
pink to meridian blue,
they'd re-do Linnaeus,

any story of black holes,
re-assign prizes
for the signature of matter,

but still they wouldn't
see what's coming.
How do I know all this?

Baby, where I come from,
we had pre-rusted pictoscopes
to tell us about aliens like you.

Saturday Night at the Firehouse

She'd had that dream again, the one
where they cleared the engine out,
ordered up gypsies with drums and *tabasi*,
and someone looking for her in the crowd.
Couldn't talk, but she knew he was there.
In real, the rubbed cement floor

with its dancing wishbone jeans
was nothing like it should've been.
Gone with the Wind. War and Peace.
Songs like *Lili Marlene.*

It wasn't she was looking for a prince.
Anyway judging from the British
princes were off. She knew
the good times come only once
or twice, matches struck in a dark,
none special if you have too many.

It was just if there'd been someone
she secretly knew was secretly
pleased she was there. No one local.
She imagined a very loose-hipped Colombian,

Jaguar Sam, all Tequila Sunrises for her
like the girl in *Goldfinger.* Hands
everywhere slowly, like a relief map
of the Great Lakes. A human volcano
that'd think he was God,
and evening squeezing into a song.

Instead, here she was
standing round in a hot allergic face
while her mind was roaring
through some night warehouse

ahead of V2 torches, desperate to match
the sea-pattern in her hands
with fabric on twenty-foot stacks.

Those gypsies were belting out
'Give me the Girl' on bamboolas
and it sounded wrong

but all the same on the ridgey floor
where the engine oil
they were all so proud of had oozed
in a stain like Madagascar, she met him,

beaked like a doctor in the plague
who enters a house with a cross on it
(marked 'God have mercy') in a leather mask,
eye-slits blocked in with glass,
gauntlets reaching to elbows,
cowslip-root pouched next the skin:

a man filled with broken light
sifting inwards like sharp fur-flakes
in a kettle. And afterwards it wasn't
at all what she imagined. But it did.

RUTH PITTER

So Good of Their Kind

'Snakes hanging from a tree!
Snakes hanging from the rough crack-willow bark!
Snakes hanging – come and see –
It almost frightened me –
I passed, and saw them shining in the dark.'

Not snakes, huge slugs. They hung
Twined in sevenfold embrace, by a tough slime;
Strong slime that held them wrung
Together, swinging and strung
In the great double helix of our time,

And there suspended, till
They had accomplished what they had to do.
And though they seemed so still
It was dynamic will
That held them, and their world about them too.

Fissured and frowning rock
Behind and overhanging, the bole seemed;
But strong desire had struck
That too; each ridge and nook
With something glittering and precious gleamed.

There must have been some dance,
Some festal wooing; for the rugged face
With nacreous phosphor glanced,
Festooned with radiance:
So they had dignified their nuptial place.

A strong electric tide
Flowed through my flesh, so honoured to have seen them:
All life was on their side,
Death was so well defied –
And then I saw a wonder grow between them.

Something – a great round gem –
Seemed from the two twined bodies to be growing;
Flower on a double stem,
The soul of both of them,
Each lost, both consummated in one knowing.

It flowered and faded: rest
Took them a moment, as they hung entwined
And vulnerable: at best
Their strength was of the least:
They had attained their height: their star declined.

One wreathed himself away,
Climbing the wonderful rope. The other soon
Devouring the strong grey
Bond of their nuptial day,
Followed, and with strange swiftness both were gone.

But one on the rough rind
Turning towards his fellow as he moved,
Eager to seek his blind
Safe crevice, yet could find
A moment for the mate whom he had loved:

With almost courtly pause,
Turning the head with almost conscious grace,
Seeming to know the laws
By which life pleads love's cause,
With the soft mouthparts touched the other's face.

H

Raspberry Nectar

The Raspberry when in full bloom is much frequented by
various species of Hymenoptera, which react to the situation
with an over-excitement often amounting to belligerence.

Why do you clash your lush plush bums together,
Rustle your sable capes and silver-banded wings,
Wild bees, tame bees, hoverflies all of a dither,
Worthy hardworking females, drudging things,
Who never seem to have any time but for the needful,
Egg-laying, nest-building, food-gathering, humdrum and heedful –
What is the siren song the Raspberry sings?

'O here is the *meaning* of lush plush bums and sable
Shoulder-capes, and the reason for silver bands,
Stripes and fandangoes, and all our blithering babble –
O now we know the Universe Understands!
We haven't a nest – we don't know where the place is!
We were born for this, not to care for our various races,
But to have a High Time, and smack one another's faces!'

Good Enthroned

Absolute good sits throned in the middle of the mind
There must be – I know there is – a heaven to find:
Our final bliss, perfectly passionate, perfectly kind:
It is our first love, long since left behind.

We need no more than one look to know our own.
Turn a page. In place of the print, an image is shown:
Then broken and healed, created and overthrown,
We fall at the feet of the New we have always known.

DEBORAH RANDALL

Nightwatchman

Brother nightwatchman I have shared your way,
black upon black footfall upon the crazily paved street
and eyes and hands full of each other so drunk
the wine to vinegar as we walk without talk on my tongue
and hands feeling for ourselves as only strangers can,

the lock and the alien roof and the fumble for them
unseemly unhomely things that we build about ourselves
after marriages have broken I still dream of eggs bitter
and raw such as my father slid down his throat at dawn,
falling from my fingers so much rage still to come,

I don't remember a time in two years when alcohol
wasn't wailing in my veins, a substitute for tears
like the grab and grind with a new nightwatchman,
the surprising angle of the apple in your throat
the lotion in your skin, you don't smell like him,

stairs are unholy alliances, every one and many
sneaking under the soles of our feet the squeak
of female philandering as I size the nightwatchman's shoulders
estimate the blades in there and how they shall
rub for pleasure under my hands two wishbones wondering,

the door is the single hymen I have to admit you
and you ahead owning me and my womb without name
flicking your beautiful hair gold and white and shampoo
and I live alone, lone as the furthest star that cannot
be seen, little girl frantically signalling,

nightwatchman on my carpet you are so naked, and proud
as a pose, I have watched this maleness, I see in the dark
and I know, and I'm tired, tired of the drumskin belly
the random muscle below, a perilous house of cards
is building in me, my history frail and impersonal,

the neon snakes of your arms nightwatchman
wind and wind about me and the carpet rolls us up
and the solitary bed is empty our flesh on the floor
in choreography, and a neighbour rapping his fifty year old
indignation, an accompaniment to my game,

I open my four lips for your fingertips and my cunt weeps
as my face won't, and like an angry sponge absorbs you,
all, and when you are sleeping I watch the night,
small boys sleep off their pleasure, I watch
the night, and wonder at such perfect death.

The Hare

The hare might almost be a concept
but is beyond thought,
quick as a cream-tailed comet,
mute as the colour brown.

The hare strips lychetts,
is blunt and gangling in play
but with a flick and a twist
leads the hounds of hell astray
over cliffs.

Pendulum-bellied cows munch ear-of-hare,
they tread hare in but hare is spring
and surfaces again further up the field.
The hare paddles the field, against
the grain of the grass.

The hare's ears swivel in weather-vanes,
register thunder, echo-sound shoals of wind,
an armada gathering in the channel.
The hare's nose tastes the many strains of air.

The hare's fur is hyperactive
and untouched in a lifetime,
soft and mysterious as moleskin,
fast as fluid.

The hare's eyes are subterranean,
earth made them,
the grass laps their glassy balls
and drowns them.

The hare is a blood-song,
a song in the blood, a shivering
up and down the spine, from a time before
words outsped their meaning.

My Favourite Sunday

Old ladies in church hats remind me of giraffes,
something about gravity slipping chins down necks
always straining for the pulpit
in wet-look straw and raw crimplene,
a squabble in their throats
and bosoms with the massive swank of rhinoceros.

Old ladies in church hats remind me of lions,
a suggestion of puffy blue heads on the prowl,
or hyenas daubed round the mouth
an expression of just having eaten a carcass.

White old ladies and that great white hunter
the vicar, on safari together,
it was invariably the young and the weak
he sniped for over the sepulchre
as we lay between the pews and played dead.

My favourite Sunday was the Sunday I chose
never to go to church again
until I was old and wanted to be
eighty per cent of the church congregation
and my own salvation then I suppose
would seem more imperative,
could no longer be said to be more
synonymous with survival.

Gael Marian

You should see my life Holy Mother,
step down out of that candle cupboard.
I can just imagine you picking through
the cow dung in our yard. I needed
a drink or two to get through my life.
To be an Irishwoman is a raw deal,
did no Irishwoman tell you?
I can see you're not a drinking woman
in your complexion, which is so pure, so how
did you dirty yourself enough to have him?
Without spot or sin, now there's a neat trick.
I used to think your father in heaven
had raped you, same as my father on earth,
but you looked too happy. My baby also
was a boy who slipped out of me
in the fields one day, a bloody fledgling
with an old stunned face, and he's still there
in snow and sun, no trouble to anyone.

If I lay on my back in bed I can see
the blue mountains. Since the old one went
I'm all that's left and the sheets clot
with all the time I spend in bed, they smell
like rotten egg with unwashing.
I can't be bothered, I think of the beach,
wide and handsome, and powder under my toes
where I ran as a child knickerless into the sea.
There'll never be that time again, it hurts me maybe.
Yesterday I was a girl, hairless, blank,
where the wind blew my brains out.
I wish thinking had come to me, and anger,
sooner, but I ate flat bread, bad-mouthed none
and kept on the run, my best freedom
to race the wind off the sea.
I wish I was a sailor, to be a sailor
is ideal, not to belong is ideal.
Sailors own the world, the sailors
I've kissed who don't care for anyone.

Down to one cow hollering to have the milk
taken off, I pity her. The priests make more mess,
they hatch and hatch in this country,
they drop their messes on the head
of a poor woman, the priests I've kissed
who don't care for anyone.
I make my own music when I've had a few,
I make a party. They must hear me roaring
in heaven but I can't be bothered to gag.
The thing about you Holy Mother
is your silence, you don't have a tongue
or a temper, by the look of you
like the top of a sea I can't get into.
It doesn't worry me, most things are over,
most of my life has run in wax
through my fingers, those idle candles
we burnt between us.

MICHÈLE ROBERTS

Magnificat
(for Sian, after thirteen years)

oh this man
what a meal he made of me
how he chewed and gobbled and sucked

in the end he spat me all out

you arrived on the dot, in the nick
of time, with your red curls flying
I was about to slip down the sink like grease
I nearly collapsed, I almost
wiped myself out like a stain
I called for you, and you came, you voyaged
fierce as a small archangel with swords and breasts
you declared the birth of a new life
in my kitchen there was an annunciation
and I was still, awed by your hair's glory

you commanded me to sing of my redemption

oh my friend, how
you were mother for me, and how
I could let myself lean on you
comfortable as an old cloth, familiar as enamel saucepans
I was a child again, pyjamaed
in winceyette, my hair plaited, and you
listened, you soothed me like cakes and milk
you listened to me for three days, and I poured
it out, I flowed all over you
like wine, like oil, you touched the place where it hurt
at night we slept together in my big bed
your shoulder eased me towards dreams

when we met, I tell you
it was a birthday party, a funeral
it was a holy communion
between women, a Visitation

it was two old she-goats butting
and nuzzling each other in the smelly fold

Madwoman at Rodmell

she strolls in the valley, alone
her ears scan the warning
twanging of birds
her boots plop and suck in the mud's grip

the sky is a cold gold spoon
sun tart and sweet
in the cup of hills licked
clean by the gulp of cows
– at the cup's lip, the foam
and crust of milk, a swell of clouds
and yellow plums; leaves curl
like the peel in marmalade

the world is her mouth
a sour swill of yells

trees scar, and suddenly
redden; bright berries of blood and teeth
hang in the hedge; the bad
baby is out; she
bites through the net; she swarms
free, fizzing; she thunders like bees in a box
maddened for honey, and her mama

her lips clang shut on mean rations:
she swallows the river
and mourns on down, a thin bellyful

Flying to Italy

The Alps are a college of grand-
mothers in white caps. Massed
profiles rear up, as pure
as nuns'.

They dandle only the air
on their scalloped laps.
Clouds infiltrate
their knees' blue valleys.

Closer, they are all
mouth: discussing
the clatter of pilots out of tin
carrycots onto these ridged tips
that snap them up, teeth
needling the lovely boys, tongues
sucking the gristle off bones.

You could easily lose your heart
to these bad grannies:
they are so possessive!

They'll cherish
the flesh of businessmen
better than any hostess, these
lipsmacking sisters; they'll
teach young wives and other
survivors how to carve up
the sun-dried dead, and eat.

We scuttle past.
Now we're only a glint
in their turquoise eye.

Patience is their vocation.

Temporarily resident

I'm living in the wrong house.

Stuck in the speechless lodgings
I hold my breath
to make the evenings pass
hearing the television
and the telephone
downstairs.

Blocked from the kitchen
by a foreign body
my hands
stitched into a thriller
keep trying
to hang up my apron
on invisible hooks.

Nobody knows the names
my best friends call me.
Nobody, politely
notices my eyes.

Neat in black linen
I smirk over drinks
at academics tight-
lipped as wallets.

My mouth kisses a cigarette
so as not to embarrass.
Paid mother, paid midwife
paid muse
to others' words.

I'm big with emptiness
as these winter fields
I pass on my way to work.

Just you and me now
I bellow to the polished coils
of broken flowerpots.

Through the mist
sunlight spreads itself
on the churned earth
cold and calm as milk.

Lacrimae rerum

Another leak
in the lavatory roof
drip drip down the lightbulb.
I pissed in the dark, raindrops
smacking my shoulder-blades.

This morning I woke
to fresh wet birdsong
under a cloud of quilt
last night's hot sweetness
still fizzing between my legs.

I was fooled into swallowing spring
jumping up to make tea
and rinse dishes, whistle
a liquid kitchen oratorio.

It's your birthday next week.
This time next year
I think you'll be gone
quietly as this water
slipping over my hands.

After your funeral
we'll return
to your parched house.
We'll try to hold our mother up
like this exhausted roof.

I carry your dying
inside me
as real as milk

as I'll carry on
getting the roof fixed
making love
weeping into the washing-up.

ANNE ROUSE

Her Retirement

Just a little party, nothing swank,
I told the founder, but you know Mr B.
There are so many of you here to thank.

I leave you the later tube trains, dank
At the hand-rails from a human sea,
Dreaming down to Morden via Bank.

I've homed quietly to port while others sank,
By keeping at my stenography.
There are so many of you here to thank.

I scan the backs of houses, rank on rank:
The comfy lamps, the oblique misery
Streaming down to Morden via Bank.

Our gardens keep us from the abyss, I think.
With the cheque I'll buy a trellis, or a tree.
There are so many of you here to thank.

And unaccustomed as I am to drink,
I toast you all who follow me
– There are so many of you here to thank –
In dreaming down to Morden, via Bank.

England Nil

The advance to Hamburg broke with all the plans.
Doug spelled them out in Luton Friday night.
Someone had ballsed it up. A dozen vans
Waited in convoy, ringside. Blue and white
We stumbled through. The beer
When we found it in that piss-hole of jerries
Was all we needed. Who won the war,

Anyway? Who nuked Dresden? Two fairies
Skittered behind the bar, talking Kraut
Or maybe Arabic. We clocked the poison
Smiles and chanted till the SS threw us out.
Stuttgart was a tea-party to this. One
By one they've nicked us, berserk with fear.
You've been Englished but you won't forget it, never.

Night Song

Our own death will be someone's
Milestone, whether we are teenaged,
Riding pillion on grown-up machines,
Or old, hoping 'they'll find a cure'.

Newscasters salt each dish with it,
The glandular fear of the secret hero,
The suicide, and the wife left to wonder
What he was thinking mid-air.

The middle-aged dears musing down
The slope of the garden to the canal
Embrace a sexy Catholicism.
A dosser drinks his last sense blurred.

It sounds at each door,
Leaving its card but it will come back
In remarkable guises, a wolf, a raven.
You will have to learn to live with it.

Like a cabin of hostages, reduced to adoring
A denimed bringer of horror or mercy, we wait,
Suspecting it's the god, the core
Out of which all, nothing is something is.

Sunset Grill

EATS blinks red onto the parking lot.
The guy's guitar lets go
But Nadine don't wanna be true, whatever.
Rolling Rock's on special.

You OK?
She was right between them when it happened.
No time to duck or nothing.

His slim brown girlfriend slips off his knees.
It ain't easy dancing on peanut shells.
Play Hot Rod Lincoln.

I worked for him once and I can tell you straight...

She writes with a felt tip on a cocktail napkin,
Hair Fair   Brookfield Plaza
Ask for Renee.
Does it look that bad? he asks, gulping his beer.

The wired stand-up base
Cools, bum-bum, and the guitar
Loves us tonight
In Virginia, raining everywhere.

The Uni-Gym

At a shout to a disco drum, the women dance
In sorbet cotton knits. Sweat darkening
On spines, they bend and reach.

In the stone chill of the gym downstairs,
Weightlifters howl, as if for sex,
Or pace, furtive in the room-sized mirror,

To meet gingerly in bed. His density
Helps him feel safer from the likes of her –
Whose heart is stronger now, and unforgiving.

CAROL RUMENS

Rules for Beginners

They said: 'Honour thy father and thy mother.
Don't spend every evening at the Disco.
Listen to your teachers, take an O level
or two. Of course, one day you'll have children.
We've tried our best to make everything nice.
Now it's up to you to be an adult!'

She went to all the 'X' films like an adult.
Sometimes she hung around the Mecca Disco.
Most of the boys she met were dead O level,
smoking and swearing, really great big children.
She had a lot of hassle with her mother;
it was always her clothes or her friends that weren't nice.

At school some of the teachers were quite nice,
but most of them thought they were minding children.
'Now Susan,' they would say, 'You're nearly adult
– behave like one!' The snobs taking O level
never had fun, never went to the Disco;
they did their homework during 'Listen with Mother'.

She said: 'I'd hate to end up like my mother,
but there's this lovely bloke down at the Disco
who makes me feel a lot more like an adult.'
He murmured – 'When I look at you, it's nice
all over! Can't you cut that old O level
scene? Christ, I could give you twenty children!'

He had to marry her. There were three children
– all girls. Sometimes she took them to her mother
to get a break. She tried to keep them nice.
It was dull all day with kids, the only adult.
She wished they'd told you that, instead of O level.
Sometimes she dragged her husband to the Disco.

She got a part-time job at the Disco,
behind the bar; a neighbour had the children.
Now she knew all about being an adult
and, honestly, it wasn't very nice.
Her husband grumbled – 'Where's the dinner, mother?'
'I'm going down the night-school for an O level,

I am,' said mother. 'Have fun at the Disco,
kids! When you're an adult, life's all O level.
Stay clear of children, keep your figures nice!'

Geography Lesson

Here we have the sea of children; here
A tiny piece of Europe with dark hair.
She's crying. I am sitting next to her.

Thirty yellow suns blobbed on cheap paper,
Thirty skies blue as a Smith's Salt-wrapper
Are fading in the darkness of this weeper.

She's Czechoslovakia. And all the desks
Are shaking now. The classroom window cracks
And melts. I've caught her sobs like chicken-pox.

Czechoslovakia, though I've never seen
Your cities, I have somehow touched your skin.
You're all the hurt geography I own.

The First Strokes
Letter to a friend learning English

Before he died, my father drowned in silence.
I thought of him just now, writing to you
In my head about the sea – that medicinal light
I longed to rush to your city of rooms and deadlines,
Your lost July – since it was he who taught me
To swim. In any sea he was stylish, fluent.
He knew its idioms, loved its argument.
So, when my four-year-old, his adventuring grandchild,
Slipped her hold on a wet rock, dropped speechless
Into the swell, he plunged and rescued her.
She used to tell us how huge fish came leering,
Making eyes at her as she bubbled down;
Now what she likes to remember are the hands
That drove apart the soupy green, and calmly
Scattered her suitors, saved her for the sun.
It was soon after this I led him to the pool:
I made him teach me. And, in half an hour,
I had left his side, was lazily at home
In the deepest water, thinking I'd always known how.
It was as simple as doing what he told me
– An obedience I could never risk as a child.
By the time he lost language, I had almost learned
To talk to him. He studied dictionaries
At first with an embarrassed grin, then frowning,
And the deep words we could have plumbed together
Ran white. I thought of all this, writing a blue
Letter about the sea, wanting to coax you
Into the tongue you almost know, but fear,
Having come so late to its stories; wanting to say
That the strokes of an English sentence are easy, requiring
Only a little self-trust as you kick off
From the margin and glide towards me, sensing all round you
The solid, patient, unbreakable arm of the water.

The Muse of Argument

At first, no more than
      A fret of breeze that twists
The fossil bracken,
      Shyness and anger twin-
Leashed to a straining wrist:
      Then she is visible
And she embodies all
      Silence that steels itself
Under a woman's heartbeat
      And stammers to take aim.
I keep back my breath
      For her, but the dart has skimmered
Already, sealed its roost
      In disarray: the sky
Plunges, heels alight
      And tightly pressed.
Plaudits, abasements die
      At her feet, with clouded looks.
And still she seems to doubt
      Her own connection.
Her shoulders are a book,
      Caught naked, trying to close,
And her face has taken on
      The colour of a wound,
      Its deep, historic rose.

Last of the Lays

Part One

At Ivalo's tyre-crazed cross-roads, snow was the sphinx
And *Murmansk* was what she murmured. One night you got restless.

(The nights were long, alas. We weren't new lovers.
'Follow me. I am your Fate' wouldn't wash any more).

I heard your foot-swords slicing the forest-fleece
With finality. Then from your breast swooped a brilliant birdman.

Choice, choice, choice gasped the wind as you gashed it.
In front of you, ghostly as lilacs, stood your live lungs.

Part Two

In Persil-white Ivalo the enemy was drink.
I had nothing to come to but a Finnish Cosmo

And nothing to read but a radioactive omelette.
My cutlery stuttered, my skis would begin any minute,

So I tacked outside into a mean minus-thirty,
And wound up at the Word, that high-lettered horror.

I turned as it told me. I plummeted and plodged
And became wild-life and expected instant extinction.

I lit on the luminous secret of synchronised movement
Momentarily, but omitted to take it with me.

I slept on my skis, and revolutionary roughnecks
Lobbed snow-lumps like one-off hand-jobs, and roamed the ice

Like spinning-tops wreathed in a frost of eye-water.

Part Three

Bang on the border, they'd opened a Super-Safeways,
Hit by recession, closed for the duration.

Some tanked-up gun-jabber jogged me: 'Nadezhda Krupskaya?'
'Crumbs!' I said. 'Wrong revolution. Julian Clary.'

Part Four

He didn't find that funny, which meant, as I'd feared,
History hadn't happened, it hadn't begun.

And though the ski-tracks still straggled under the *Push* sign
They were being disexisted at serious speed.

This was the hairiest I had ever imagined:
Me, on God's side, just about. You, back on the other:

The border, bristling. Remember those terrible games
– When the sound's switched off, there's got to be someone dancing,

And the grin's de rigeur, because English losers are laughers?
I hope, wherever you're harboured, you look like a natural

– Straight bck, heels tgthr, bm on chr –
I hope when it thaws and the home-thoughts unfreeze our faces,

Whoever I am I'll
                    author an honest tear.

EVA SALZMAN

The English Earthquake

Somewhere, a cup tinkles in its saucer.
A meek 'oh my' passes down the miles
of manicured gardens, as armies rumble

the monuments of cities continents away.
The budgie chirps 'goodness' to thin air
while Bach quivers slightly and the fat roast

sways in the oven, brain-dead, but chuckling
in its oil. Such a surprise: the settling ground,
innocent with rape and mustard, groaning

under its weight of roses. The premier
sees stars, plumps her pillows for photographs.
Alas, *Watchtower* faces are falling as life goes on

and the Ex-Major winds back years to the war –
its incendiary thrill – his wife flushed
with disbelief as the earth moves unexpectedly,

the giant baby at the core of the planet
rocking its apocalyptic cradle
gently, wailing: 'Hungry, hungry, hungry.'

The Refinery

You cannot look at narrow-brush moustaches.
You cannot think about gas-cookers, their ovens
flame-rimmed, the diadem of fire, or hear the bell
when it's done. Or think of teeth, lamp-shades, soap,
the refinery chimney-stacks, puffing cheerfully.

You cannot raise your hand in history class
to ask a simple question; your arm freezes
in a parody of salute. You cannot write 'horror'
because horror is a good film for anyone
with a strong stomach and a taste for gore.

Anyway, the antique photographs are grainy,
have blurred into art – that vaseline trick with the lens.

At dinner you sip the rot-gut wine
and listen to the table-talk – an operation botched
or an ache in the joints the doctor couldn't diagnose.
You choke with rage at the meal, gibbering,
while the devil samples your soul like buttered croissant.

Time Out

Imagine there being no exacting word for time,
there being nothing to waste or save, invent
or slip away. Then who would fight the crime
of its fast passing? I'd take, say, the three-cigarette

train departing half-past-after-the-last-word
which wants saying (and not a moment too soon!)
while the numberless dial of my watch would refer
to a changing mise-en-scène winding from sun to moon,

or some event to an eventual end, when a black 'For Hire'
drives me home on its own good time. *Good* time. For tides
aren't for living by, but are only there to admire
occasionally on trips to the timeless seasides.

Nor do we milk cows, farm a natural time, say to friends:
'I'll meet you at the end of this cooking of rice'
or, more vaguely still: 'You know...when the afternoon ends'.
When? Would I be on time, guided by a smoky feel of night,

when it fell, in my bones – another made-up clocking-in machine?
But how would I measure these purposeful distances run,
or almost run, as the case would more likely seem?
The racers might just laugh or chat at the starting-gun.

Some joke, infernal time! Not a word, not well-made policy,
but some black jester's dressed-up devastating game
which lets me put off the proverbial plot, infinitely,
so I could wait here forever before you finally came, or not.

Conch

My grandmother doesn't hear me call; a white mist licks
her skull. She shuffles out to the jungle-yard
to pin a single greying cloth to the drying rack's
sun-dial spines, the dulling weather-vane
where the fading laundry's years have swung and aired.

The piece of washing turns its only two pages
back and forth, re-read by the wind, water veins
mapping the ground, while shadows throw vaguer
and vaguer epitaphs across the sheets snapping in the breeze.
The woman goes inside, and her door shuts again
into the memory I'll always hold of its splintered frieze.

But my real grandmother's sealed thousands of miles away
in her red-brick house deafened with treasure – bone-and-tulle
dancing skirts, dried quills, the family of bells
lined up in ever-decreasing size, their peals subsiding
to white noise, her shell collection emptying the sea,
vowels bleached on another shore; and from the countless shelves
she's taken her umpteenth book to read in bed, yearning
for me, for the children, her ears burning.

CAROLE SATYAMURTI

My First Cup of Coffee

I'm sophisticated in my Cuban heels,
my mother's blue felt hat
with the smart feather like a fishing fly

as I sit with her in the Kardomah; and
coffee please, I say, not orange squash,
crossing my legs, elegant as an advert.

Beyond the ridges of my mother's perm
the High Street is a silent film
bustling with extras: hands grasping purses,

steering prams, eyes fixed on lists,
bolster hips in safe-choice-coloured skirts
– and then, centre screen, Nicolette Hawkins

(best in the class at hockey, worst at French)
and a boy – kissing,
blouse straining, hands

where they shouldn't be:
the grown-up thing. My hat's hot, silly;
coffee tastes like rust.

My mother, following my gaze, frowns: common.
I'm thinking, if I could do all that
I could be bad at French.

Feast of Corpus Christi: Warsaw

The line snail-ribbons
down Krakowskie Street – women,
girls, some medalled veterans.
Slow hymns, as for a funeral;
crowds press, voices join in,
a helicopter tacking overhead.

The procession swerves,
passes the crucifix of flowers
made secretly one night, by women:
flowers as witness,
candles for endurance,
lumps of coal for solidarity.

Candles in jars, steady in the draught;
soldiers with Modigliani faces.
Is it their grandmothers
who bring fresh flowers each day,
work them in calmly, eyes lowered
as their knees roughen on stone?

It could be their sisters,
surge of first-communion white,
who know the hymns by heart,
who bear these banners
embroidered with an image from the East:
a Madonna, black as coal.

Sex Object

The Romanies are gone.
No longer eyesore, blot, threat, health hazard,
they're off, leaving a scatter of plastic,
heaps of rusty parts,
the smell of woodsmoke.

But in the small hours,
one steals into Jenny Wilson's bed
and lifts her nightdress.
Oh, she murmurs, as his grimy hand
strokes her thigh, testing,
as though he'd rubbed it down with wire wool.
She gleams in the moonlight
ready for further renovation.

His brush is silken. It drips
with fire, smells of molten chocolate.
Flame flows into every hole and crack.
How did I not know this before, she says.

And now, the polishing,
soft, sweet-smelling wax.
He massages her shoulders, hips,
with circular caresses.
She is a race horse,
a Chinese cabinet,
a centuries-old newel post.
Her skin is milk, and steel.

And now – but now it's daylight.
Eyes open on her ordinary room.
She's stretching, thinking – these days
ideological unsoundness
is the most delicious sin there is.

Ghost Stations

We are the inheritors. We hide here
at the roots of the perverted city
waiting, practising the Pure Way.
Listening to ourselves, each other,
we find the old soiled words won't do;
often we can only dance our meanings.

Deep in the arteries of London, life
is possible – in the forgotten stations:
York Road, St Mary's, Seething Lane...
I love the names. Each day, we sing them
like a psalm, a celebration
– Down Street, British Museum, City Road.

We live on waste. After the current's off
we run along tunnels, through sleeping trains,
ahead of the night cleaners. We find chips,
apple cores (the most nutritious part),
dregs of Coke. On good days, we pick up
coins that fit the chocolate machines.

Once I found a whole bag of shopping.
That night we had an iceberg lettuce,
a honeydew melon, tasting of laughter.
And once, an abutilon – its orange
bee-flowers gladdened us for weeks.
Such things are dangerous;

then, to remind ourselves, we read
the newspapers we use as mattresses.
Or gather on the platforms,
witness the trains as they rip past
(our eyes have grown used to the speed).
Almost every known depravity

is acted out on trains – rape, drunkenness,
robbery, fighting, harassment, abuse.
And the subtler forms – intellectual bullying,
contempt, all the varieties of indifference...
We've learned to read the faces;
we need to see these things, simply.

The travellers only see their own reflections.
But lately, a few in such despair
they cup their faces to the glass, weeping,
have seen the ghost stations
and though we're always out of sight,
they sense our difference and find their way.

Our numbers are growing, though there are
reverses. Some lose heart, want to leave.
We can't let them – we keep them all
at Brompton Road, carefully guarded,
plotting uselessly, swapping fantasies,
raving of sunlight, mountains or the sea.

One day, we'll climb out, convert the city!
The trains are full of terrible energy;
we only have example, words. But there is
our chant to strengthen us, our hope-names:
Uxbridge Road, King William Street,
South Kentish Town, South Acton, Bull and Bush...

E.J. SCOVELL

A Woman Condemned to Virtue

From future time the grey flowed into her hair
As the light flowed into her mirror from outer space.
She looked in the mirror and saw her mother there.

'It is only a trick of light, the snow in the air...
But how shall I live my life, wearing her face?'
From future time the grey flowed into her hair

While antique voices chimed how alike they were,
For words half heard may find their time and place:
She looked in the mirror and saw her mother there.

'But she stays home-bound, gentle and wise in her chair,
And I am the wild one that runs a dangerous race.'
From future time the grey flowed into her hair,

And the impartial winter light laid bare
In the bones of her skull a genetic calm and grace.
She looked in the mirror and saw her mother there.

We range less far than we think and from anywhere
May round the world to a long relinquished base.
From future time the grey flowed into her hair:
She looked in the mirror and saw her mother there.

The New House
FROM *Three Poems in Memory of a Child*

The new unfinished house
Had an emptiness, notwithstanding
The dusty garden soil
Brought in on feet or with winding
Of air through the window louvres,
And the florid heat abounding,
And the bell voices of children
Constantly sounding
Sweetly now, now clanging
Untimed; and with coming and going
The doors in the gusts banging.

The new inchoate house
Which the present and future filled
Had an emptiness, that held
The absence of the child,
The quiet one, never here.
And pain, unreconciled,
Drifting like air, dishevelled
The furnishing, and like stirring
Of earth had cracked the flooring:
Pain that can fracture the ground
Of a life beyond all curing.

This was before they had roofed
And walled with a lacy low
Parapet the verandah,
And planted quick to grow
Hibiscus, passion fruit,
And reclaimed the slope below
With pineapples and hardy
Root-crops and the rainfall tree.
This was while goats grazed free
Still over grass and thorns
And the litter of masonry.

But in those days, on the open
Verandah, work done, and cooled
The air and the thirsty land,
When the sun had dropped and the wild
Children had dropped like stones,
When they were still and were spread
Like wonders in shop windows
On the coverless sheet of the bed –
On the verandah, when light
From indoors fell soft as shade
And the voices of adults strayed,

Or the moon freed from the mountain
Poured equal light on the land,
The seaward fields and the sea's
Plains and long arc beyond –
On the sea and the unreclaimed
Land such quiet lay
As if the quiet child
Had taken her absence away;
Or as if the touch of the air
And the kindness of beauty and light
Had been news of her.

Deaths of Flowers

I would if I could choose
Age and die outwards as a tulip does;
Not as this iris drawing in, in-coiling
Its complex strange taut inflorescence, willing
Itself a bud again – though all achieved is
No more than a clenched sadness,

The tears of gum not flowing.
I would choose the tulip's reckless way of going;
Whose petals answer light, altering by fractions
From closed to wide, from one through many perfections,
Till wrecked, flamboyant, strayed beyond recall,
Like flakes of fire they piecemeal fall.

The Paschal Moon

At four this April morning the Easter moon –
Some days to full, awkwardly made, yet of brazen
Beauty and power, near the north-west horizon
Among our death-white street lamps going down –
I wondered to see it from a lower storey
Netted in airy twigs; and thought, a fire
A mile off, or what or who? But going higher
I freed it (to my eyes) into its full glory,
Dominant, untouched by roofs, from this height seen
Unmeshed from budding trees; not silver-white
But brazed or golden. Our fluorescent light,
That can change to snow a moment of young green
In the maple tree, showed ashen, null and dead
Beside such strength, such presence as it had.

J

JO SHAPCOTT

Lies

In reality, sheep are brave, enlightened
and sassy. They are walking clouds
and like clouds have forgotten
how to jump. As lambs they knew.
Lambs jump because in their innocence
they still find grass exciting.
Some turf is better for tiptoeing
say the lambs. Springy meadows
have curves which invite fits
of bouncing and heel-kicking
to turn flocks of lambs
into demented white spuds boiling in the pot.
Then there is a French style of being a lamb
which involves show and a special touch
at angling the bucking legs. Watch carefully
next time: Lambs love to demonstrate –
you won't have to inveigle.
Eventually, of course, lambs grow trousers
and a blast of wool
which keeps them anchored to the sward.
Then grass is first and foremost
savoury, not palpable.
I prefer the grown sheep: even when damp
she is brave, enlightened and sassy,
her eye a kaleidoscope of hail and farewell,
her tail her most eloquent organ of gesture.
When she speaks, it is to tell me
that she is under a spell, polluted.
Her footwear has been stolen
and the earth rots her feet.
In reality she walks across the sky
upside down in special pumps.

Goat

Dusk, deserted road, and suddenly
I was a goat. To be truthful it took
two minutes, though it seemed sudden,
for the horns to pop out of my skull,
for the spine to revolutionise and go
horizontal, for the fingers to glue
together and for the nails to become
important enough to upgrade to hoof.
The road was not deserted any more, but full
of goats, and I liked that, even though I hate
the rush hour on the tube, the press of bodies.
Now I loved snuffling behind his or her ear,
licking a flank or two, licking and snuffling here,
there, wherever I liked. I lived for the push
of goat muscle and goat bone, the smell of goat fur,
goat breath and goat sex. I ended up on the edge
of the crowd where the road met the high
hedgerow with the scent of earth, a thousand
kinds of grass, leaves and twigs, flower-heads
and the intoxicating tang of the odd ring-pull
or rubber to spice the mixture. I wanted
to eat everything. I could have eaten the world
and closed my eyes to nibble at the high
sweet leaves against the sunset. I tasted
that old sun and the few dark clouds
and some tall buildings far away in the next town.
I think I must have swallowed an office block
because this grinding enormous digestion tells me
it's stuck on an empty corridor which has
at the far end, I know, a tiny human figure.

Muse

When I kiss you in all the folding places
of your body, you make that noise like a dog
dreaming, dreaming of the long runs he makes
in answer to some jolt to his hormones,
running across landfills, running, running
by tips and shorelines from the scent of too much,
but still going with head up and snout
in the air because he loves it all
and has to get away. I have to kiss deeper
and more slowly – your neck, your inner arm,
the neat creases under your toes, the shadow
behind your knee, the white angles of your groin –
until you fall quiet because only then
can I get the damned words to come into my mouth.

Phrase Book

I'm standing here inside my skin,
which will do for a Human Remains Pouch
for the moment. Look down there (up here).
Quickly. Slowly. This is my own front room

where I'm lost in the action, live from a war,
on screen. I am an Englishwoman, I don't understand you.
What's the matter? You are right. You are wrong.
Things are going well (badly). Am I disturbing you?

TV is showing bliss as taught to pilots:
Blend, Low silhouette, Irregular shape, Small,
Secluded. (Please write it down. Please speak slowly.)
Bliss is how it was in this very room

when I raised my body to his mouth,
when he even balanced me in the air,
or at least I thought so and yes the pilots say
yes they have caught it through the Side-Looking

Airborne Radar, and through the J-Stars.
I am expecting a gentleman (a young gentleman,
two gentlemen, some gentlemen). Please send him
(them) up at once. This is really beautiful.

Yes they have seen us, the pilots, in the Kill Box
on their screens, and played the routine for
getting us Stealthed, that is, Cleansed, to you and me,
Taken Out. They know how to move into a single room

like that, to send in with Pinpoint Accuracy, a hundred Harms.
I have two cases and a cardboard box. There is another
bag there. I cannot open my case – look out,
the lock is broken. Have I done enough?

Bliss, the pilots say, is for evasion
and escape. What's love in all this debris?
Just one person pounding another into dust,
into dust. I do not know the word for it yet.

Where is the British Consulate? Please explain.
What does it mean? What must I do? Where
can I find? What have I done? I have done
nothing. Let me pass please. I am an Englishwoman.

Motherland
(after Tsvetayeva)

Language is impossible
in a country like this. Even
the dictionary laughs when I look up
'England', 'Motherland', 'Home'.

It insists on falling open instead
three times out of the nine I try it
at the word 'Distance' –
degree of remoteness, interval of space –

the word is ingrained like pain.
So much for England and so much
for my future to walk into the horizon
carrying distance in a broken suitcase.

The dictionary is the only one
who talks to me now. Says laughing,
'Come back HOME!' but takes me
further and further away into the cold stars.

I am blue, bluer than water
I am nothing, for all I do
is pour syllables over aching brows.

England. It hurts my lips to shape
the word. This country makes me say
too many things I can't say, home
of my rotting pride, my motherland.

PENELOPE SHUTTLE

Jungian Cows

In Switzerland, the people call their cows
Venus, Eve, Salome, or Fraulein Alberta,
beautiful names
to yodel across the pastures at Bollingen.

If the woman is busy with child or book,
the farmer wears his wife's skirt
to milk the most sensitive cows.

When the electric milking-machine arrives,
the stalled cows rebel and sulk
for the woman's impatient skilful fingers
on their blowzy tough rosy udders,
will not give their milk;

so the man who works the machine
dons cotton skirt, all floral delicate flounces
to hide his denim overalls and big old muddy boots,
he fastens the cool soft folds carefully,
wraps his head in his sweetheart's sunday-best fringed scarf,
and walks smelling feminine and shy among the cows,

till the milk spurts, hot, slippery and steamy
into the churns,
Venus, Salome, Eve, and Fraulein Alberta,
lowing, half-asleep,
accepting the disguised man as an echo of the woman,
their breath smelling of green, of milk's sweet traditional climax.

Alice

I live in one room.
My bedroom is my kitchen,
my study is my bathroom.
I am absorbed by my own powers,
feeling beautiful and resourceful.
I am awaiting an avalanche of young.
In me fifteen new hearts beat.
My stretched belly-skin is near splitting,
my bulk is pastoral, I know.
I smell of melons and cheese.
I am not restless or nervous.
I look pityingly at you
who don't possess my one room.
Soon there will be such a squall of piglet,
a shoal of tails and tingling ears,
an april fall of flesh,
a sixty-legged blind creature,
not a scratch on it;
a chute of pig, shriller than puppies,
fitter than fleas. I know all this
from previous experience.
Every one of my imminent litter will possess
our breed's gift for caricature.
The dog will turn and run from their chaos.
They will not be dangerous in their cherry-pale
and sugar-bright skins; but loud.
In the paddock they will race and scamper.
Like mine, their lives will be immensely public.
Under the afternoon sky they will sleep
as babyishly as in any cartoon
that would bonnet and bib them,
as if their flesh were lifelong safe, inedible,
and myself, Alice, their mother,
a human mother resting with full breasts bared
and aching in the flickering shade of the mimosa tree.

Five Carp, Two Swans

The big heads of five saffron carp rise from the pond,
indecent-lipped, impressionistic and impish,
their scaled shoulders fond of the weight of water,
coarsely-glimmering in the sandy six-inch shallows;
their slothful aunt-like eyes watch our blue shadow hands
stretched out to them in as deep a languor as theirs;
like sucklings they slubber up cake from our fingers,
their lips delicately-snarling, pinkly-raddled;
they graze on bread from my daughter's flat cautious palm
without tickling, tender as ponies.
They are like tasting souls, lifting gourmet heads above water,
testing nature's heart on this side, air too bright,
but food so fine.
We could feed them anything, plums, dog biscuits, bananas,
but in glinting unison, a hand of fishes, they shoal and slither
to the darker centre of the rippled pool,
as one black honeymooning swan females towards us,
her eye vain, cool and greedy, jostling air with her lipstick-red beak;
we poke the last of our picnic crossly into its dry cochineal clack.

With fin de siècle certainty she rejoins her watching mate,
fossil-black wings folded, grey paddle-feet idling;
the swans share silence, their marriage is mute,
their long-necked love is made of circling,
of drifting towards night, of being black,
of going grandly on the water, fish belching beneath their feet.

Your Girl

Not knowing you are a horse, your girl gives you a glass of wine.
Not knowing you are a horse, she flies through your gloom
on a cloud of family flowers.
Your girl takes your life in her hands,
lighter than a bird of glass her breath trustingly manufactures.
She has not fallen in love with a horse.
She comes to you because you are frail and human.

You sleep with her in a low and lacquered chinese bed,
on silk-fringed pillows of peony and sunflower,
under a water-lilied and willow-treed quilt of satin.
On the wall, an intimate embroidery
of Aphrodite contemplating her youngest child,
drowsy and triumphant on his mother's couch...
(You embrace under the oriental covers,
the lamp calmly-shawled in its stiff-eyeletted shade of white card
throwing a ruff of shadow on her face...)

The night knows you are a horse
but your girl does not, despite her wisdom, her honesty,
her unselfish and amorous mouth, her skin sheer as white poppies.
What a fabric she is for stitching, you are the thread
moving in her, your tears hidden from her.
Such a sigh you draw from her, like water from the river in Egypt,
Nile flood, heaven caught in the net of her sex,
her own smell sudden rain on leaves and brambles,
or the blue necks of doves.

Then she sleeps in the dazed bed.
She sleeps in your arms, your girl, your bedouinne.
She dreams you are a horse.
She dreams she forgives you
and that she canters through favourite rooms on your strong wide
          back.

PAULINE STAINER

The Elderbrides

It was the day
She first noticed
Her breasts growing.

She sat on the summer-house step;
Felt them tilt
Through her slip.

They shook
Under the cambric,
White does in shade.

It was then
She smelled the elderflower;
The gypsy-blooms,

The rank-dreamers
Who shake out shawls
For the dead.

They trembled above her head,
Five-petalled, five-stamened,
Vibrant in the breeze,

And suffused her body,
Fleeting, equivocal,
In bridal with the stealing sun.

Piranesi's Fever

It could have been malaria –
the ricochet of the pulse
along his outflung arm,
grappling-irons
at each cautery-point on the body.

She lay with him between bouts;
pressed to his temple
the lazy estuary of her wrist;
brought him myrrh
on a burning salver.

How lucid they made him,
the specifics against fever:
the magnified footfall of the physician,
the application of cupping-glasses
above the echoing stairwell,

windlass and shaft,
the apparatus of imaginary prisons;
a catwalk slung across the vault
for those who will never take
the drawbridge to the hanging-garden.

None of this he could tell her –
that those he glimpsed
rigging the scaffold
were not fresco-painters,
but inquisitors giddy from blood-letting;

that when he clung to her
it wasn't delirium
but a fleeting humour of the eye –
unspecified torture,
death as an exact science.

Only after each crisis, could he speak
of the sudden lit elision
as she threw back the shutters
and he felt the weight of sunlight
on her unseen breasts.

The Water Glass

As children,
We dipped the surplus summer eggs
In waterglass for wintering;

Layered them pointed-end down,
Lightly tiered
In the cold of the slippery jar.

We would reach down to our armpits,
Through a shivered kingdom
Of refracted shells.

Above the magnified ivory,
Our faces floated on the ruffled surface,
Plumped-out or skeletal,

Apparitions of tension –
The ritual of unreal children
In a dangerous glass.

Cocteau and the Equilibrist

He watches me, even at rehearsals,
brooding over
the imagined applause,
the glisten of sweat
on the nape of my neck.

I am Barbette
transvestite rope-walker,
my soles sensitive
as those of Chinese Women
wading naked for jade.

I wear weightless silk
of a blue that lightens
at dusk,
dance to multiple shadows
as if accompanied.

How casual I make it seem –
the controlled tremor
between movements,
the act
timed to perfection.

I never meet his gaze;
but after the last glissade
when I push past him
the rope burns again
between my thighs.

Xochiquetzal

The firefighters of Chernobyl
lie naked
on sloping beds
in sterile rooms,
without eyelashes
or salivary glands

o death
take them lightly
as the Colombian goddess
who makes love
to young warriors
on the battlefield

holding a butterfly
between her lips.

ANNE STEVENSON

The Spirit is too Blunt an Instrument

The spirit is too blunt an instrument
to have made this baby.
Nothing so unskilful as human passions
could have managed the intricate
exacting particulars: the tiny
blind bones with their manipulating tendons,
the knee and the knucklebones, the resilient
fine meshings of ganglia and vertebrae
in the chain of the difficult spine.

Observe the distinct eyelashes and sharp crescent
fingernails, the shell-like complexity
of the ear with its firm involutions
concentric in miniature to the minute
ossicles. Imagine the
infinitesimal capillaries, the flawless connections
of the lungs, the invisible neural filaments
through which the completed body
already answers to the brain.

Then name any passion or sentiment
possessed of the simplest accuracy.
No. No desire or affection could have done
with practice what habit
has done perfectly, indifferently,
through the body's ignorant precision.
It is left to the vagaries of the mind to invent
love and despair and anxiety
and their pain.

The Marriage

They will fit, she thinks,
but only if her backbone
cuts exactly into his rib cage,
and only if his knees
dock exactly under her knees
and all four
agree on a common angle.

All would be well
if only
they could face each other.

Even as it is
there are compensations
for having to meet
nose to neck
chest to scapula
groin to rump
when they sleep.

They look, at least,
as if they were going
in the same direction.

Swifts

Spring comes little, a little. All April it rains.
The new leaves stick in their fists. New ferns, still fiddleheads.
But one day the swifts are back. Face to the sun like a child
You shout, 'The swifts are back!'

Sure enough, bolt nocks bow to carry one sky-scyther
Two hundred miles an hour across fullblown windfields.
Swreeeee. Swreeee. Another. And another.
It's the cut air falling in shrieks on our chimneys and roofs.

The next day, a fleet of high crosses cruises in ether.
These are the air pilgrims, pilots of air rivers...
But a shift of wing and they're earth-skimmers, daggers,
Skilful in guiding the throw of themselves away from themselves.

Quick flutter, a scimitar upsweep, out of danger of touch, for
Earth is forbidden to them, water's forbidden to them.
All air and fire, little owlish ascetics, they outfly storms.
They rush to the pillars of altitude, the thermal fountains.

Here is a legend of swifts, a parable –
When the great Raven bent over earth to create the birds
The swifts were ungrateful. They were small muddy things
Like shoes, with long legs and short wings, so

They took themselves off to the mountains to sulk.
And they stayed there. 'Well,' said the Raven, after years of this
'I will give you the sky, you can have the whole sky
On condition that you give up rest.'

'Yes, yes,' screamed the swifts. 'We abhor rest.
We detest the filth of growth, the sweat of sleep,
Soft nests in the wet fields, slimehold of worms.
Let us be free, be air!'

So the Raven took their legs and bound them into their bodies.
He bent their wings like boomerangs, honed them like knives.
He streamlined their feathers and stripped them of velvet.
Then he released them, *Never to Return*

Inscribed on their feet and wings. And so
We have swifts, though in reality not parables but
Bolts in the world's need, swift
Swifts, not in punishment, not in ecstasy, simply

Sleepers over oceans in the mill of the world's breathing.
The grace to say they live in another firmament.
A way to say the miracle will not occur,
And watch the miracle.

Making Poetry

'You have to inhabit poetry
if you want to make it.'

And what's 'to inhabit'?

To be in the habit of, to wear
words, sitting in the plainest light,
in the silk of morning, in the shoe of night;
a feeling, bare and frondish in surprising air;
familiar...rare.

And what's 'to make'?

To be and to become words' passing
weather; to serve a girl on terrible
terms, embark on voyages over voices,
evade the ego-hill, the misery-well,
the siren hiss of *publish, success, publish,*
success, success, success.

And why inhabit, make, inherit poetry?

Oh, it's the shared comedy of the worst
blessed; the sound leading the hand;
a wordlife running from mind to mind
through the washed rooms of the simple senses;
one of those haunted, undefendable, unpoetic
crosses we have to find.

Talking Sense to my Senses

Old ears and eyes, so long my patient friends,
For you this silicon nerve and resin lens.
Guides when I heard and saw, yet deaf and blind
Stumbled astray in the mazes of my mind,
Let me assist you now I've lived to see
Far in the dark of what I have to be.

Shunted outside the hubbub of exchange,
Knowledge arrives, articulate and strange,
Voice without breath, light without sun or switch
Beamed from the pulse of an old awareness which
Tells me to age by love and not to cling
To ears, eyes, teeth, knees, hands – or any thing.

And even then,

there may be a language in which
memory will be called 'letting in the sorrow'.
It would be a black language.
The sorrow would be a rainbow
after the storm, at its beginning.

Music in this language would mean
'measuring the rhythms', and poetry,
'translating the dreams'.
Power? A hush in which to honour
winds' work, and the sun's.

A long litany of astonishment
would be, in this language,
a hymn of thanksgiving: 'Even as it died,
the sea made power out of its own pulse,
pounding to salt the poisoned cities
of the suicides.'

BIOGRAPHICAL NOTES

Fleur Adcock was born in 1934 in Papakura, New Zealand. She read Classics at Victoria University, Wellington, and emigrated to Britain in 1963. She is a freelance writer and translator, and lives in London. Her *Selected Poems* appeared from Oxford University Press in 1983, followed by *The Incident Book* (1986) and *Time-Zones* (1991). Her translations include books by the Romanian poets Grete Tartler and Daniela Crăsnaru for OUP, and *The Virgin & the Nightingale* (1983), a collection of medieval Latin lyrics, for Bloodaxe.

Gillian Allnutt was born in 1949 in London. Her collections include *Beginning the Avocado* (Virago, 1987) and *Blackthorn* (Bloodaxe, 1994). She is the author of *Berthing: A Poetry Workbook* (NEC/ Virago, 1991) and co-editor of *The New British Poetry* (Paladin, 1988). She was for some years poetry editor of *City Limits*, and now works as a freelance writer and tutor. She lives near Durham.

Moniza Alvi was born in 1954 in Lahore, Pakistan. She was joint winner of the Poetry Business Competition in 1991. Her first full collection, *The Country at My Shoulder* (OUP, 1993), was a Poetry Book Society Recommendation. She lives and teaches in south London.

Nuala Archer was born in 1955 in New York of Irish parents. She has lived in Ireland and in North, Central and South America. She has published three collections, *Whale on the Line* (Gallery, 1981), *Two Women, Two Shores*, with Medbh McGuckian (Salmon, 1989) and *Pan/Ama* (Salmon, 1992).

Annemarie Austin was born in 1943 in Devon and grew up on the Somerset Levels and in Weston-super-Mare, where she lives today. Her first collection *The Weather Coming* (Taxus, 1987) was a Poetry Book Society Recommendation; her second, *On the Border*, was published by Bloodaxe in 1993.

Leland Bardwell was born in 1928 in India. She grew up in Leixlip, Co. Kildare, and then travelled widely, living in London and Paris during the 1940s and 1950s; she now lives in Co. Sligo. She studied Ancient History at the University of London as an extramural student, and has worked as a translator in Paris and Budapest. She is also a novelist and playwright. Her latest book *Dostoevsky's Grave: New & Selected Poems* (Dedalus, 1991) draws on work from previous collections including *The Mad Cyclist* (1970) and *The Fly and the Bed Bug* (1984).

Elizabeth Bartlett was born in 1924 in Kent. She worked as a medical secretary for 16 years, and later in the home help service and as a tutor. She lives in Burgess Hill, Sussex. Her books include *A Lifetime of Dying* (Peterloo, 1979), *Strange Territory* (Peterloo, 1982), *The Czar Is Dead* (Rivelin, 1986), *Instead of a Mass* (Headland, 1991) and *New & Selected Poems* (Bloodaxe, 1994).

Patricia Beer was born in 1919 in Exmouth. She taught English Literature at Padua University in Italy and at Goldsmith's College, London, then left teaching in 1968 to become a full-time writer. She lives in Devon. Her poetry books include *Collected Poems* (1988) and *Friend of Heraclitus* (1993), both published by Carcanet.

Connie Bensley was born in 1929 in London. She is a freelance writer. She published two collections with Peterloo, *Progress Report* (1981) and *Moving In* (1984), and *Central Reservations: New & Selected Poems* (1990) and *Choosing To Be a Swan* (1994) with Bloodaxe.

Sujata Bhatt was born in 1956 in Ahmedabad, India, and educated in the USA. She lives in Germany where she works as a freelance writer and as a translator of Gujarati poetry into English. She has published three collections with Carcanet, *Brunizem* (1988), *Monkey Shadows* (1991) and *The Stinking Rose* (1994).

Eavan Boland was born in 1944 in Dublin, where she works as a reviewer and lecturer. Her books include *The War Horse* (1975), *In Her Own Image* (1980) and *Night Feed* (1982) from Arlen House, and *The Journey* (1987), *Selected Poems* (1989), *Outside History* (1990) and *In a Time of Violence* (1994) from Carcanet. Her pamphlet *A Kind of Scar: The Woman Poet in a National Tradition* was published in the LIP series by Attic Press, Dublin, in 1989.

Alison Brackenbury was born in 1953 in Lincolnshire. She read English at Oxford, and worked for some years as a librarian. She is now an electro-plater, living in Cheltenham. She has published four books of poetry with Carcanet: *Dreams of Power* (1981), *Breaking Ground* (1984), *Christmas Roses* (1988) and *Selected Poems* (1991).

Jean 'Binta' Breeze was born in 1956 in Jamaica. She is a poet, playwright, actress, dancer and choreographer, and divides her time between London and the Caribbean. Her collections include *Riddym Ravings* (Race Today, 1988) and *Spring Cleaning* (Virago, 1992).

Heather Buck was born in 1926 in Greenhithe, Kent. She began writing in 1966 and now lives in Suffolk. Her collections *At the Window* (1982), *The Sign of the Water Bearer* (1987) and *Psyche Unbound* (1994) are published by Anvil.

Eiléan Ní Chuilleanáin was born in 1942 in Cork and lives in Dublin, where she teaches at Trinity College and co-edits *Cyphers*. She is published by Gallery in Ireland and by Bloodaxe in Britain, her books including *The Second Voyage: Selected Poems* (Gallery/Bloodaxe, 1986) and *The Magdalene Sermon* (Gallery, 1989).

Gillian Clarke was born in 1937 in Cardiff and has lived in Wales most of her life. She is a broadcaster, freelance writer and lecturer. She edited the *Anglo-Welsh Review* from 1975 to 1984. Her books *Letter from a Far Country* (1982), *Selected Poems* (1985), *Letting in the Rumour* (1989) and *The King of Britain's Daughter* (1993) are published by Carcanet.

Wendy Cope was born in 1945 in Erith, Kent. She read History at Oxford, and worked for many years as a teacher. She is a free-lance writer, and lives in London. Her books include two poetry collections from Faber, *Making Cocoa for Kingsley Amis* (1986) and *Serious Concerns* (1992), a collection of finger rhymes for children, *Twiddling Your Thumbs* (Faber, 1988), a poet-artist collaboration with Nicholas Garland, *The River Girl* (Faber, 1991), and an anthology of women's poetry for teenagers, *Is That the New Moon?* (Collins, 1989).

Jeni Couzyn was born in 1942 in South Africa. She grew up in Johannesburg, and studied at the University of Natal. Her poetry books include *Life by Drowning: Selected Poems* (1985) and *In the Skin House* (1993), both from Bloodaxe. She edited *The Bloodaxe Book of Contemporary Women Poets* (1985) and the Livewire teenage anthology *Singing Down the Bones* (Women's Press, 1989). She is a psychotherapist, and lives in London.

Hilary Davies was born in 1954 in London, and read French and German at Oxford, where she co-founded *Argo*. She now teaches modern languages in a London school and is currently Chair of the Poetry Society. Her first collection *The Shanghai Owner of the Bonsai Shop* was published by Enitharmon in 1991. In 1992 she edited a special women's poetry issue of *Aquarius* magazine.

Nuala Ní Dhomhnaill was born in 1952 in Lancashire, and grew up in the West Kerry Gaeltacht (Irish-speaking area). She lives in Dublin. Her books include *Selected Poems/Rogha Dánta* (translated by Michael Hartnett, Raven Arts, 1986), *Pharoah's Daughter* (various translators, Gallery, 1990) and *The Astrakhan Cloak* (translated by Paul Muldoon, Gallery, 1992).

Maura Dooley was born in 1957 in Truro, Cornwall, and grew up in Bristol. She has worked for the Arvon Foundation at Lumb Bank and the South Bank Centre in London, and is currently Artistic Director of Swansea City of Literature 1995. Her first book-length collection, *Explaining Magnetism* (Bloodaxe, 1991), was a Poetry Book Society Recommendation.

Freda Downie was born in 1929 in London, and educated in Britain and Australia. She worked for music publishers and art agents for many years, and only began publishing her poems in the 1970s, in limited editions; two full collections, *A Stranger Here* (1977) and *Plainsong* (1981), followed from Secker. She died in 1993.

Carol Ann Duffy was born in 1955 in Glasgow. She grew up in Staffordshire, later moved to Liverpool, and now lives in London, where she is a freelance writer. She edited the Kestrel anthology *I Wouldn't Thank You for a Valentine* (Viking, 1992), and has published four collections with Anvil: *Standing Female Nude* (1985), *Selling Manhattan* (1987), *The Other Country* (1990) and *Mean Time* (1993).

Helen Dunmore was born in 1952 in Yorkshire. After studying English at York University, she taught in Finland for two years. She is a freelance writer of poetry, short stories, poems for children and novels, and lives in Bristol. She has published four collections, all with Bloodaxe: *The Apple Fall* (1983), *The Sea Skater* (1986), *The Raw Garden* (1988) and *Short Days, Long Nights: New and Selected Poems* (1991); her other books include a novel, *Zennor in Darkness*, published by Viking in 1993.

Jean Earle was born in 1909 in Bristol, grew up in the Rhondda Valley, and has lived in various parts of Wales for most of her life, latterly near Shrewsbury. Her stories and articles appeared early in her career, but she published her first book, *A Trial of Strength* (Carcanet, 1980), when she was 71, and has since published three further collections with Seren (Poetry Wales Press), *Visiting Light* (1987), *The Intent Look* (1984) and *Selected Poems* (1990).

U.A. Fanthorpe was born in 1929 in Kent, and educated at Oxford. Until she made a mid-career switch and took a job as a clerk in a Bristol hospital, she taught at Cheltenham Ladies' College for many years. She is now a freelance writer and lives in Gloucestershire. Her *Selected Poems* (Peterloo, 1986) is published in paperback by Penguin, and she has published five other collections with Peterloo, most recently *A Watching Brief* (1987) and *Neck-Verse* (1992).

Vicki Feaver was born in 1943 in Nottingham, and read Music at Durham University and English at University College London. She lives in London and works in Chichester, teaching English and Creative Writing at the West Sussex Institute. Her first collection, *Close Relatives*, was published by Secker in 1981; her second is due from Cape in 1994.

Elaine Feinstein was born in 1930 in Lancashire. After reading English at Cambridge, she worked for Cambridge University Press, and taught at the University of Essex. She is a freelance writer, and lives in London. Her collections include *The Celebrants* (1973), *Some Unease and Angels: Selected Poems* (1977), *Badlands* (1986) and *City Music* (1990), all from Hutchinson. She has translated Russian poets including Marina Tsvetayeva, and has published several novels. She won a Cholmondeley Award in 1990.

Elizabeth Garrett was born in 1958 in London and grew up in the Channel Islands. Since completing her D.Phil. at Oxford University on the Fool in modern English and French poetry, she has worked in the Bodleian Library and for the Voltaire Foundation. She lives in Oxford. Her first book-length collection, *The Rule of Three*, was published by Bloodaxe in 1991.

Pamela Gillilan was born in London, ran a decorating business in Cornwall for many years, and now lives in Bristol. She won the Cheltenham Festival poetry competition in 1979 after writing no poetry for 25 years. Her poetry books are published by Bloodaxe: *That Winter* (1986), shortlisted for the Commonwealth Poetry Prize; *The Turnspit Dog* (1993), a collaboration with artist Charlotte Cory; and *All-Steel Traveller: New & Selected Poems* (1994).

Lavinia Greenlaw was born in 1962. She grew up in Essex, and in London where she lives. She has worked in publishing as an editor and now works for the London Arts Board. Her publications include *The Cost of Getting Lost in Space* (Turret, 1991), *Love from a Foreign City* (Slow Dancer, 1992) and *Night Photograph* (Faber, 1993).

Rita Ann Higgins was born in 1955 in Galway, Ireland, and still lives there. She was Galway County's Writer-in-Residence in 1987, and received a Peadar O'Donnell Award in 1989. Her poetry books, all published by Salmon, are: *Goddess & Witch* (1990), which combines *Goddess on the Mervue Bus* (1986) and *Witch in the Bushes* (1988); and *Philomena's Revenge* (1992). Her plays include *Face Licker Come Home* (1991), *God of the Hatch Man* (1992) and *Colie Lally Doesn't Live in a Bucket* (1993).

Selima Hill was born in 1945 in London, and grew up on a farm. She read Moral Sciences at Cambridge. She has spent most of her life working with children, and now lives in Dorset. She won the Arvon/*Observer* International Poetry Competition in 1988 with part of her book-length poem *The Accumulation of Small Acts of Kindness* (Chatto, 1989). Her other books of poetry are *Saying Hello at the Station* (Chatto, 1985), *My Darling Camel* (Chatto, 1988), *A Little Book of Meat* (Bloodaxe, 1993), and *Trembling Hearts in the Bodies of Dogs* (Bloodaxe, 1994).

Frances Horovitz was born in 1938 in London. She read English and Drama at Bristol, trained as an actress, and worked as a broadcaster and performer of poetry, and as a poetry tutor. She published four collections of poems, including *Water Over Stone* (Enitharmon, 1980) and *Snow Light, Water Light* (Bloodaxe, 1983). She died in 1983, aged 45, after a long illness. Her *Collected Poems* was published by Bloodaxe in 1985.

Kathleen Jamie was born in 1962 in Renfrewshire, grew up in Midlothian, and now lives in Fife, where she is a freelance writer. She has travelled around the East, the fruits of which include two poetry books from Bloodaxe, *The Way We Live* (1987) and *The Autonomous Region* (with Sean Mayne Smith, 1993), and a travel book, *The Golden Peak* (Virago 1992). She has also published *A Flame in Your Heart* (Bloodaxe, 1986), a book of poems set in the summer of 1940, written with Andrew Greig. Her latest collection is *The Queen of Sheba* (Bloodaxe, 1994).

Elizabeth Jennings was born in 1926 in Boston, Lincolnshire. She went to school and university in Oxford, where she has lived for most of her life. She won a Somerset Maugham Award for her second book of poems, *A Way of Looking* (1955), which enabled her to travel to Italy. She drew upon 17 collections of poetry for her *Collected Poems 1953-1985* (Carcanet, 1986), which won the W.H. Smith Literary Award. Her latest collections from Carcanet are *Tributes* (1989) and *Times and Seasons* (1992). She also published a book on mystical poetry, *Every Changing Shape* (1961).

Jenny Joseph was born in 1932 in Birmingham. She is a freelance writer, and lives in Gloucestershire. Her *Selected Poems* (Bloodaxe, 1992) includes work from four previous collections, including *The Thinking Heart* (1978) and *Beyond Descartes* (1983). Her other books include: *Persephone* (Bloodaxe, 1986), a fiction in prose and poetry, winner of the James Tait Black Memorial Prize, and *Beached Boats* (Enitharmon, 1991), with photographer Robert Mitchell.

Sylvia Kantaris was born in 1936 in Derbyshire, lived in Australia for some years, and now lives in Helston, Cornwall, where she is a freelance writer. Her books of poems include *Dirty Washing: New & Selected Poems* (Bloodaxe, 1989) and her latest collection *Lad's Love* (Bloodaxe, 1993), as well as two collaborations, *News from the Front* with D.M. Thomas, and *The Air Mines of Mistila* (Bloodaxe, 1988) with Philip Gross (Poetry Book Society Choice).

Jackie Kay was born in 1961 in Edinburgh, grew up in Glasgow, and now lives in London, where she is a freelance writer. She has written three plays, two poetry collections, *The Adoption Papers* (Bloodaxe, 1991) and *Other Lovers* (Bloodaxe, 1993), and a collection of poetry for children, *Two's Company* (Blackie, 1992), winner of the Signal Poetry Award. Her poem-film *Twice Through the Heart* was shown in the BBC 2 *Words on Film* series in 1992.

Mimi Khalvati was born in 1944 in Tehran, and was educated in Britain and Switzerland. She worked as an actress and a director of the Theatre Workshop, Tehran, translating from English into Farsi and devising new plays, and later co-founded the Theatre in Exile group. Her first collection, *In White Ink*, was published by Carcanet in 1991. She lives in London.

Liz Lochhead was born in 1947 in Motherwell, Lanarkshire, and apart from two years in America has spent most of her adult life in Glasgow. She trained as a painter at Glasgow School of Art, and worked as an art teacher for eight years. Her publications include *Dreaming Frankenstein and Collected Poems* (Polygon, 1982), *True Confessions and New Clichés*, a set of monologues and theatre pieces (Polygon, 1985), and *Bagpipe Muzak* (Penguin, 1991). She has written several plays for stage, radio and TV.

Marion Lomax was born in 1953 in Newcastle, grew up in Northumberland, and now lives in Berkshire. She gained her doctorate from the University of York in 1983, and her study of Elizabethan and Jacobean drama was published by CUP in 1987. Her first book of poems, *The Peepshow Girl*, appeared from Bloodaxe in 1989. She lectures in English at St Mary's College, Strawberry Hill.

Medbh McGuckian was born in 1950 in Belfast, studied at Queen's University, Belfast, and was later writer-in-residence there. She won first prize in the National Poetry Competition in 1979. Her first three books were published by OUP: *The Flower Master* (1982), *Venus and the Rain* (1984) and *On Ballycastle Beach* (1988). Her latest collection, *Marconi's Cottage*, was published in Ireland in 1991 by Gallery and in Britain in 1992 by Bloodaxe.

Paula Meehan was born in 1955 in Dublin. She runs workshops in prisons, schools, universities and with community groups throughout Ireland. She has published three collections of poetry, *Return and No Blame* (1984) and *Reading the Sky* (1986) from Beaver Row, and *The Man Who Was Marked by Winter* (Gallery Press, 1991).

Elma Mitchell was born in 1919 in Airdrie, Scotland. She is a professional librarian and has worked in broadcasting, publishing and journalism in London. She now lives in Somerset. She has had four books of poetry published by Peterloo Poets: *People Etcetera: Poems New & Selected* (1987) includes work from two earlier collections, *The Poor Man in the Flesh* (1976) and *The Human Cage* (1979); a subsequent book, *Furnished Rooms* (1983), is out of print.

Grace Nichols was born in 1950 in Guyana, where she grew up, and has lived in Britain since 1977. She won the Commonwealth Poetry Prize in 1983 for her poem cycle *i is a long memoried woman* (Karnac House), and has since published a novel, *Whole of a Morning Sky* (1986), and two collections, *The Fat Black Woman's Poems* (1984) and *Lazy Thoughts of a Lazy Woman* (1989), all with Virago. Her books for children include two collections of stories, a book of poems and two anthologies. She lives in Lewes in Sussex.

Julie O'Callaghan is an American-born poet who lives in Ireland. Born in Chicago in 1954, she settled in Dublin in 1974, and works in the Library of Trinity College. Her first collection, *Edible Anecdotes* (Dolmen Press, 1983), was a Poetry Book Society Recommendation, and her second, *What's What* (Bloodaxe, 1991), was a Poetry Book Society Choice. Her children's poems are published by OUP and by Orchard in her book *Taking My Pen for a Walk* (1990).

Ruth Padel was born in 1944. She researched Greek tragedy, religion and psychology in Oxford, Paris, Berlin and Athens, teaching in London, Crete, and on the sponge-divers' island of Kalymnos. She now lives in London, finishing a book on madness, *Whom Gods Destroy*, to follow *In and out of the Mind* (Princeton University Press, 1992). She has published two books of poems, *Summer Snow* (Hutchinson, 1990) and *Angel* (Bloodaxe, 1993).

Ruth Pitter was born in Ilford in 1897. In 1955 she became the first woman to receive the Queen's Gold Medal for Poetry, and was made a CBE in 1979. Her *Collected Poems* (Enitharmon, 1990) includes work from many collections published from 1934 to 1975, as well as *A Heaven to Find* (1987), a selection of unpublished work written between 1908 and 1976. She was known to a wide audience through the TV *Brains Trust*. She died in 1992.

Deborah Randall was born in 1957 in Hampshire, and now lives in Ullapool in Scotland. In 1987 she won first prize in the Bloodaxe and Bridport poetry competitions. She has published two collections with Bloodaxe, *The Sin Eater* (1989), which won a Poetry Book Society Recommendation and a Scottish Arts Council Book Award, and *White Eyes, Dark Ages* (1993).

Michèle Roberts was born in 1949 in England, and is half French. She lives mainly in London. She has been poetry editor of *Spare Rib* and *City Limits*. Her publications include two books of poems from Methuen, *The mirror of the mother* (1986) and *Psyche and the hurricane* (1990), and six novels, *A Piece of the Night* (1978), *The Visitation* (1983), *The Wild Girl* (1984), *The Book of Mrs Noah* (1987), *In the Red Kitchen* (1990), and *Daughters of the House* (1992), which was shortlisted for the 1992 Booker Prize and won the W.H. Smith Literary Award in 1993.

Anne Rouse was born in 1954 in Washington, DC, and grew up in Virginia. After reading History at the University of London, she worked as a general and psychiatric nurse, and became active in trade unionism, as a NUPE steward, and in local health politics. Since 1986 she has worked for a mental health charity in London. Her first collection of poems, *Sunset Grill* (Bloodaxe, 1993), was a Poetry Book Society Recommendation.

Carol Rumens was born in 1944 in London. She has been poetry editor of *Quarto* and *The Literary Review*, and has held several writing fellowships, most recently at Queen's University, Belfast. Her latest book *Thinking of Skins: New & Selected Poems* (Bloodaxe, 1993) includes work from seven previous collections. She has also written short stories, plays and a novel, *Plato Park* (1987).

Eva Salzman was born in 1960 in New York, and grew up in Brooklyn where, from the age of 10 until 22, she was a dancer and later a choreographer. She moved to Britain in 1985, taught dance and exercise, and set up an out-of-print book search service run from her home in Brighton. Her first book of poems, *The English Earthquake* (Bloodaxe, 1992), was a Poetry Book Society Recommendation.

Carole Satyamurti was born in 1939 and grew up in Kent. She lived in America, Singapore and Uganda before settling in London, where she teaches at the University of East London. She won first prize in the National Poetry Competition in 1986, and has since published two collections with OUP, *Broken Moon* (1987) and *Changing the Subject* (1990).

E.J. Scovell was born in 1907 in Sheffield, and lives in Oxford. She has worked as an ecological field assistant in Brazil and Panama, and has often visited the Antilles. Her first book of poems came out in 1944. Her *Collected Poems* (1988) and *Selected Poems* (1991) are published by Carcanet.

Jo Shapcott was born in 1953 in London. She has been an English lecturer, an education officer, and currently works for Music Theatre Forum in London. She is the only poet to have won first prize in the National Poetry Competition twice, in 1985 and (jointly) 1991. She has published two collections, *Electroplating the Baby* (Bloodaxe, 1988) and *Phrase Book* (OUP, 1992), and is currently editing an anthology of contemporary Slovenian poetry for Bloodaxe.

Penelope Shuttle was born in 1947 in Middlesex, and now lives in Falmouth, where she is a freelance writer. She has published five collections with OUP: *The Orchard Upstairs* (1980), *The Child-Stealer* (1983), *The Lion from Rio* (1986), *Adventures with my Horse* (1988) and *Taxing the Rain* (1992). She has also published several novels and *The Wise Wound: Menstruation and Everywoman*, with Peter Redgrove (Gollancz, 1978; HarperCollins, 1994).

Pauline Stainer was born in 1941 in Stoke-on-Trent, and read English at Oxford. Before taking an M.Phil. at Southampton University, she worked in a mental hospital, a pub and a library. She now lives at Little Easton, Dunmow, Essex. She has published three collections with Bloodaxe, *The Honeycomb* (1989), *Sighting the Slave Ship* (1992) and *The Ice-Pilot Speaks* (1994).

Anne Stevenson was born in 1933 in Cambridge of American parents. She grew up in New England and in Ann Arbor, studied music and languages at the University of Michigan, and returned to Britain in 1954. After living in London, Oxford, Cambridge, Glasgow, Dundee, Hay-on-Wye and Co. Durham, she has now settled in Wales. Her *Selected Poems 1956-1986* (OUP, 1987) includes work from seven previous books; her latest collections from OUP are *The Other House* (1990) and *Four and a Half Dancing Men* (1993). She has also published a study of the American poet Elizabeth Bishop, and a biography of Sylvia Plath, *Bitter Fame* (Viking, 1989).

ACKNOWLEDGEMENTS

Thanks are due to the following copyright holders for permission to publish the poems in this anthology:

Fleur Adcock: To author and Oxford University Press Ltd for poems from *Selected Poems* (1983), *The Incident Book* (1986) and *Time-Zones* (1991): © Fleur Adcock 1983, 1986, 1991.

Gillian Allnutt: To author for poems from *Beginning the Avocado* (Virago, 1987) and *Blackthorn* (Bloodaxe Books, 1994): © Gillian Allnutt 1987, 1993.

Moniza Alvi: To author and Oxford University Press Ltd for poems from *The Country at My Shoulder* (1993): © Moniza Alvi 1993.

Nuala Archer: To author and The Gallery Press for poems from *Whale on the Line* (1981): © Nuala Archer 1981.

Annemarie Austin: To author for 'Nightbus' from *The Weather Coming* (Taxus, 1987); to author and Bloodaxe Books Ltd for poems from *On the Border* (1993): © Annemarie Austin 1987, 1993.

Leland Bardwell: To author for poems from *Dostoevsky's Grave* (Dedalus Press, 1991): © Leland Bardwell 1991.

Elizabeth Bartlett: To author for poems from *A Lifetime of Dying* (Peterloo Poets, 1979), *The Czar Is Dead* (Rivelin Grapheme, 1986) and *Instead of a Mass* (Headland, 1991), and for 'Themes for Women': © Elizabeth Bartlett 1979, 1986, 1991, 1993.

Patricia Beer: To author and Carcanet Press Ltd for poems from *Collected Poems* (1988): © Patricia Beer 1988.

Connie Bensley: To author and Bloodaxe Books Ltd for poems from *Central Reservations* (1990); to author for 'Politeness': © Connie Bensley 1990, 1993.

Sujata Bhatt: To author and Carcanet Press Ltd for poems from *Brunizem* (1988) and *Monkey Shadows* (1991): © Sujata Bhatt 1988, 1991.

Eavan Boland: To author and Carcanet Press Ltd for poems from *The Journey* (1987) and *Selected Poems* (1989): © Eavan Boland 1987, 1989.

Alison Brackenbury: To author and Carcanet Press Ltd for poems from *Dreams of Power* (1981) and *Christmas Roses* (1988): © Alison Brackenbury 1981, 1988.

Jean 'Binta' Breeze: To author and Virago Press Ltd for poems from *Spring Cleaning* (1992): © Jean 'Binta' Breeze 1992.

Heather Buck: To author and Anvil Press Poetry Ltd for poems from *At the Window* (1982) and *The Sign of the Water Bearer* (1987): © Heather Buck 1982, 1987.

Eiléan Ní Chuilleanáin: To author and The Gallery Press for poems from *The Second Voyage* (Gallery/Bloodaxe, 1986) and *The Magdalene Sermon* (Gallery, 1989): © Eiléan Ní Chuilleanáin 1986, 1989.

Gillian Clarke: To author and Carcanet Press Ltd for poems from *Selected Poems* (1985), *Letting in the Rumour* (1989) and *The King of Britain's Daughter* (1993): © Gillian Clarke 1985, 1989, 1993.

Wendy Cope: To author and Faber & Faber Ltd for poems from *Making Cocoa for Kingsley Amis* (1986): © Wendy Cope 1986.

Jeni Couzyn: To author and Bloodaxe Books Ltd for poems from *Life by Drowning* (1985): © Jeni Couzyn 1985.

Hilary Davies: To author and the Enitharmon Press for poems from *The Shanghai Owner of the Bonsai Shop* (1991): © Hilary Davies 1991.

Nuala Ní Dhomhnaill: To author, translators and The Gallery Press for poems from *Pharaoh's Daughter* (1990): © Nuala Ní Dhomhnaill 1981, 1984, 1990, © Eiléan Ni Chuilleanáin and Medbh McGuckian 1990.

Maura Dooley: To author and Bloodaxe Books Ltd for poems from *Explaining Magnetism* (1991); to author for 'Does It Go Like This?' and 'The Celestial Announcer': © Maura Dooley 1991, 1993.

Freda Downie: To David Turner for poems from *A Stranger Here* (Secker & Warburg, 1977): © Freda Downie Estate 1977, 1993.

Carol Ann Duffy: To author and Anvil Press Poetry Ltd for poems from *Standing Female Nude* (1985), *Selling Manhattan* (1987), *The Other Country* (1990) and *Mean Time* (1993): © Carol Ann Duffy 1985, 1987, 1990, 1993.

Helen Dunmore: To author and Bloodaxe Books Ltd for poems from *Short Days, Long Nights: New & Selected Poems* (1991); to author for 'Three Ways of Recovering a Body': © Helen Dunmore 1991, 1993.

Jean Earle: To author and Seren Books for poems from *Selected Poems* (1990): © Jean Earle 1990.

U.A. Fanthorpe: To author and Peterloo Poets for poems from *Selected Poems* (1986) and *Neck-Verse* (1992): © U.A. Fanthorpe 1986, 1992.

Vicki Feaver: To author for poems from *Crab Apple Jelly* (Somers Press, 1992) and for 'Judith', reprinted from *The Independent on Sunday*: © Vicki Feaver 1992, 1993.

Elaine Feinstein: To author and Random House UK Ltd for poems from *Badlands* (Hutchinson, 1986) and *City Music* (Hutchinson, 1990): © Elaine Feinstein 1986, 1990.

Elizabeth Garrett: To author and Bloodaxe Books Ltd for poems from *The Rule of Three* (1991): © Elizabeth Garrett 1991.

Pamela Gillilan: To author and Bloodaxe Books Ltd for poems from *That Winter* (1986) and *The Turnspit Dog* (1993): © Pamela Gillilan 1986, 1993.

Lavinia Greenlaw: To author and Faber & Faber Ltd for poems from *Night Photograph* (1993): © Lavinia Greenlaw 1993.

Rita Ann Higgins: To author for poems from *Goddess & Witch* (Salmon, 1990) and *Philomena's Revenge* (Salmon, 1992): © Rita Ann Higgins 1990, 1992.

Selima Hill: To author for poems from *Saying Hello at the Station* (Chatto, 1984) and *My Darling Camel* (Chatto, 1988); to author and Bloodaxe Books Ltd for poems from *A Little Book of Meat* (1993): © Selima Hill 1984, 1988, 1993.

Frances Horovitz: To Roger Garfitt and Bloodaxe Books Ltd for poems from *Collected Poems* (1985): © Frances Horovitz Estate 1985.

Kathleen Jamie: To author and Bloodaxe Books Ltd for poems from *The Way We Live* (1987) and *The Queen of Sheba* (1994): © Kathleen Jamie 1987, 1993.

Elizabeth Jennings: To author and David Higham Associates Ltd for poems from *Collected Poems 1953-1985* (Carcanet, 1986): © Elizabeth Jennings 1986.

Jenny Joseph: To author and John Johnson (Authors' Agent) Ltd for poems from *Selected Poems* (Bloodaxe Books, 1992): © Jenny Joseph 1992.

Sylvia Kantaris: To author and Bloodaxe Books Ltd for poems from *Dirty Washing* (1989) and *Lad's Love* (1993): © Sylvia Kantaris 1989, 1993.

Jackie Kay: To author and Bloodaxe Books Ltd for poems from *The Adoption Papers* (1991) and *Other Lovers* (1993): © Jackie Kay 1991, 1993.

Mimi Khalvati: To author and Carcanet Press Ltd for poems from *In White Ink* (1991): © Mimi Khalvati 1991.

Liz Lochhead: To author and Polygon Books for poems from *Dreaming Frankenstein & Collected Poems* (1982): © Liz Lochhead 1982.

Marion Lomax: To author and Bloodaxe Books Ltd for poems from *The Peepshow Girl* (1989); to author for 'Beyond Men': © Marion Lomax 1989, 1993.

Medbh McGuckian: To author and The Gallery Press for poems from *The Flower Master* (1982) and *Venus and the Rain* (1984), both originally published by Oxford University Press; and for poems from *Marconi's Cottage* (Gallery, 1991; Bloodaxe, 1992): © Medbh McGuckian 1982, 1984, 1991, 1992, 1993.

Paula Meehan: To author and The Gallery Press for poems from *The Man who was Marked by Winter* (1991): © Paula Meehan 1991.

Elma Mitchell: To author and Peterloo Poets for poems from *People Etcetera: Poems New & Selected* (1987): © Elma Mitchell 1987.

Grace Nichols: To author and Virago Press Ltd for poems from *Lazy Thoughts of a Lazy Woman* (1989); to author for 'Blackout', reprinted from *New Poetry 2* (British Council, 1993): © Grace Nichols 1989, 1993.

Julie O'Callaghan: To author and Bloodaxe Books Ltd for poems from *What's What* (1991): © Julie O'Callaghan 1991.

Ruth Padel: To author and Random House UK Ltd for 'Amniocentesis' from *Summer Snow* (Hutchinson, 1990); to author and Bloodaxe Books Ltd for poems from *Angel* (1993): © Ruth Padel 1990, 1993.

Ruth Pitter: To Enitharmon Press and the Ruth Pitter Estate for poems from *Collected Poems* (1990): © Ruth Pitter Estate 1990, 1993.

Deborah Randall: To author and Bloodaxe Books Ltd for poems from *The Sin Eater* (1989): © Deborah Randall 1989.

Michèle Roberts: To author and Methuen Ltd for poems from *The mirror of the mother* (1986) and *Psyche and the hurricane* (1990): © Michèle Roberts 1986, 1990.

Anne Rouse: To author and Bloodaxe Books Ltd for poems from *Sunset Grill* (1993): © Anne Rouse 1993.

Carol Rumens: To author and Bloodaxe Books Ltd for poems from *Thinking of Skins: New & Selected Poems* (1993): © Carol Rumens 1993.

Eva Salzman: To author and Bloodaxe Books Ltd for poems from *The English Earthquake* (1992): © Eva Salzman 1992.

Carole Satyamurti: To author and Oxford University Press Ltd for poems from *Broken Moon* (1987) and *Changing the Subject* (1990): © Carole Satyamurti 1987, 1990.

E.J. Scovell: To author and Carcanet Press Ltd for poems from *Collected Poems* (1988): © E.J. Scovell 1988.

Jo Shapcott: To author and Bloodaxe Books Ltd for 'Lies' from *Electroplating the Baby* (1988); to author and Oxford University Press Ltd for poems from *Phrase Book* (1992); to author for 'Motherland': © Jo Shapcott 1988, 1992, 1993.

Penelope Shuttle: To author and David Higham Associates Ltd for poems from *Adventures with My Horse* (Oxford University Press, 1988): © Penelope Shuttle 1988.

Pauline Stainer: To author and Bloodaxe Books Ltd for poems from *The Honeycomb* (1989), *Sighting the Slave Ship* (1992) and *The Ice-Pilot Speaks* (1994): © Pauline Stainer 1989, 1992, 1993.

Anne Stevenson: To author and Oxford University Press Ltd for poems from *Selected Poems 1956-1986* (1987) and *The Other House* (1990): © Anne Stevenson 1987, 1990.